The Reminiscences

of

Colonel Ruth Cheney Streeter

U.S. Marine Corps Reserve (Retired)

Interviews conducted by
John T. Mason
on behalf of
Columbia University

Interview with Mrs. Ruth Cheney Streeter
(Mrs. Thomas W. Streeter, Sr.
At her home, Morristown, New Jersey
April 30, 1979
By John T. Mason, Jr.

Q: Well, Mrs. Streeter, I'm delighted to meet you. You're such a vital charming person and have had such an illustrious career that I'm very happy to have this opportunity to talk with you and have you review this career for us.

I wonder if you'd begin in a very proper way by telling me something about your family background, for this has direct bearing on your characteristics as a person and your achievements. Would you begin in this way?

Mrs. Streeter: I'd be very glad to, Mr. Mason. It's a pleasure to have you out here, and we've provided you with a lovely spring day.

Q: You have indeed.

Mrs. Streeter: A flowering crabapple tree, and all of the things that ought to be visible and appropriate to the 30th of April.

I did, of course, have ancestors, so I presume -

Q: And rather illustrious ones.

Streeter: Well, colorful ones anyhow. My mother-in-law, and of course actually I can't borrow too much from her, but she had a lovely family biography in which she selected her ancestors very carefully, between the ones that she liked and the ones that she didn't like. Some of the ones that she liked were some of the more colorful, if not to say questionable ones, but in any case it made a very good history.

Of the ancestors who are most clear in my recollection, the first one is Benjamin Pierce Cheney.

Q: Whose dates are 1815-1895.

Streeter: That's right, and he was my father's father. They came from New Hampshire, his family did, from Hillsboro, New Hampshire, and his father was the village blacksmith at the little crossroads right near Hillsboro. The squire who lived there was President Pierce's father and he had a great big house, which is now the property of the state of New Hampshire, and it had a ballroom. This was out in the backwoods, mind you, but this was a crossroads, and the father, the squire, put up all the notables that came by the crossroads and entertained them.

Q: Almost like an inn.

Streeter: Yes, except that it was - well, it wasn't exactly - yes, I'd call it a mansion. It really was a mansion.

And it was very hospitable, and a very pleasant place.

Well, as I say, my great-grandfather was the village blacksmith. Always reminds me of Longfellow's poem. He was a hard working honest man, but it was a hard life, you know, and they had several children, the oldest of whom was my grandfather, Benjamin Pierce Cheney.

When he was born, his father asked the squire if he might name him after him, Benjamin Pierce. So that's how he came by that name. And the squire was so pleased with this attention that he gave them a ewe and a couple of lambs, and this was like money in the bank in those days. The ewe in due time produced more lambs, and there was beginning to be a little flock.

Then along came hard times, and it was a cold hard winter and there was very little for anybody to eat; and they didn't have welfare in those days, and so the lambs had to be slaughtered and eaten, one by one. And this was a tragedy.

Q: I know. I know it is.

Streeter: Well, time went one, and they weathered the hard winter somehow, and at the age of about 10, my grandfather was of course only a young boy at that time, was put out to work. And he was sort of the handy boy around the inn in Hillsboro, which was a coaching stop. It was his job to wake people up when it was time to get up and catch the coach. Ladies in those days had a great deal of trouble getting dressed in time, and they wore corsets, and because he was only a young boy, they had him come in and tighten the corsets. So he did all kinds of odd jobs, and grew up in that atmosphere. Of course by this time he knew a good deal about horses. He had a natural feel for horses, and between working in his father's blacksmith shop and working around the stagecoaches, he naturally grew up with the ambition of being a stage coach driver -- which in truth he became, when he became old enough to. And many details about this, you will find in the book I got together, partly from my grandmother's reminiscences, which is part of this collection.

He had always apparently a real reputation for reliability, and so people not only entursted their young daughters to him, to take back and forth to school, but they entrusted valuable small parcels such as watches or jewelry, things like that, which they wanted to be sure would be honestly delivered. And he used to put them inside his tall coachman's hat on top of his head, and he always claimed that was why it became prematurely bald, because the parcels rubbed all the hair off the top of his head.

Q: Well, I question that.

Streeter: In any case, he established a good reputation, and he apparently had a pretty good time on the way. In this book you will find the account of the Coachman's Ball, which occurred once a year in Concord, New Hampshire, and was of course the event of the season.

Grandpa, having observed the importance of small packages, and delivery, reliable delivery of various things as well as mail, started something called the Concord-Montreal Express, which developed and grew, and in due time grew into the American Express Company, small letters, and into transcontinental express and railroad activities.

But while he was still in New Hampshire, he was involved in a very bad train accident. A train was wrecked and two or three people were badly hurt, including my grandfather, whose right arm was broken really up to the shoulder. And of course they were out in the middle of the country. It was the crossing of a road. Didn't know how they were going to get a doctor. When who should come along but the country doctor in his horse and buggy. Just happened to be in the neighborhood.

So he took care of Grandpa, and what he did was to take off his arm right up to the shoulder joint.

Q: Rather than take care of the break, he took it off?

Streeter. It was too badly broken to save, I think. This was an unusual operation. So from then on - I think Grandpa, was about 40 at the time, you'll find it all in the book - but from then on of course he had an empty sleeve. But this didn't hold him back any.

He had a very interesting life, which I will not go into in detail now because you can find it by looking in the book of reminiscences. But he became a millionaire several times over, had his ups and downs, as did the people who put their money into transcontinental railroads in those days; but he ended up by marrying my grandmother. She was only 25 and he was 50 by that time. He had been too busy to get married until he was 50 years old.

Q: Too busy making money.

Streeter: That's right. Not making money so much as at least getting up a little bit from the extreme poverty which he knew in his youth. And they had five children. My uncle, who was B. P. Cheney, Jr. - no, my Aunt Alice, Mrs. Baltzell, was the eldest daughter, than my uncle,

B. P. Cheney, Jr., then my aunt, Mrs. Carl Kaufmann, my Aunt Lillie. She married a Swiss by the name of Carl Kaufmann. And she and Grandma came back to Peterborough, which is near Hillsboro. They had a lovely place, my grandmother did, on a ridge above the town of Peterborough, looking across to Mt. Monadnock, and my father and mother bought a piece of land on that same ridge, just beyond them, and intended to build there; but my father succumbed to tuberculosis when he was only 27 years old. My mother eventually built a beautiful house there, and that's where my two brothers and I grew up.

So that is more or less the story of that side of the family. My mother's side of the family came from Connecticut. She was born in New Britain, Connecticut. Her father was a country doctor, and he also was a good judge of horse flesh, because country doctors had to have fast horses to get where they were going, to see their patients.

There was a tragedy in this family too. We needn't think that all the accidents happen in automobiles. They had a grade crossing in New Britain, and it was supposed to have gates that went up and down when the train was coming. Well, Mother was driving her father and mother down the main street one day, and the crossing guard was drunk. He had not put the gates down. The train popped out from behind the buildings and hit the carriage and my grandmother was killed. My mother was slightly injured but not too badly and my grandfather was not hurt.

But after all that, she was anxious to get an education, and she went up to Plattsburg, New York to the normal school and was there for a year or so. From there she transferred to Wellesley College, and while she was at Wellesley, in the town of Dover which was next to Wellesley, was the home of my other grandfather. That's where she and my father met and became engaged.

He was a Harvard man, class of '92, and he'd been to St. Paul's School. Of course they naturally had no idea of getting married while he was still in college. Furthermore no idea of getting married till he had a job after he got out of college.

Q: Had to support a wife, after all.

Streeter: And was able to support a wife. And this was fortunate, because at once when they married they had babies, and my older brother and I and my younger brother were all born within five years of each other. This kept my mother very busy.

Q: You might note the fact that her name was Mary Ward Lyon, and that her dates are 1868-1943.

Streeter: Yes. That's right. Well, unfortunately, my father's health began to fail. The climate of Boston is not very good. It's very raw and wet, and apparently he had acquired tuberculosis at some stage of the game, which people didn't know very much about, how to take care of, in those days, but it was thought that if he could go out West where it was dry and sunny, that he might get over it.

Q: That was the cure in that time.

Streeter: That's right. And at that time my mother of course was pregnant with my younger brother, and so for a few months she stayed in Boston, and Father and a friend of his, Mr. Halsell went out to Colorado Springs.

But then it became evident that he was not getting any better, so Mother and all of us moved out there and my grandmother bought us a house there. And the last time I was out there, a few years ago, that house was still there, great big rambling house, and I think it has become a fraternity house for the college, in Colorado Springs.

I can remember Colorado Springs as a child, because we used to go back there from time to time, and of course, the great character in Colorado Springs was General Palmer. He founded Colorado Springs.

Well, General Palmer was the head of the Denver and

Rio Grande. My grandfather —

Q: He was an Army general, was he?

Streeter: Oh yes, he had been, in the Civil War, and my grandfather of course was a director of the Atchison, Topeka and Santa Fe Railroad And they had the war, the war between the two railroads, which you can look up in the history books if you want to know. They were both I think trying to build to the Royal Gorge, and the great question, who was going to get there first, and a few guns were trotted out, and it was a real do.

Nevertheless, Grandpa had died of course by the time that we moved out, and General Palmer couldn't have been nicer to my mother. He and his family had this great place in Colorado Springs, and they were very kind and thoughtful of Mother, who was of course having this very difficult time, because my father died three weeks after my youngest brother was born.

Q: Oh, my.

Streeter: Yes. This was a bad time, for Mother. Well, after that, Mother didn't remarry for a good many years.

Q: Did she stay in Colorado?

Streeter: No, she came back to Boston. She went to Peterborough in the summertime and she built this beautiful house up on the land that she and Father had bought, which is where I grew up. But then in the winters she was of course by this time a very wealthy and attractive young widow, and she had no desire to settle down in Boston right away, and so we traveled, for some years.

Q: The entire family?

Streeter: The entire family, and she had gotten a classmate of hers from the normal school in Plattsburg to come down and live with us, and as we grew old enough to be taught, have lessons, she taught us, and we didn't have to go to school in these various places we went to.

The first place we went to was Baltimore. We spent two winters, two consecutive winters, in Baltimore.

Q: What was the attraction in Baltimore?

Streeter: Well, she had friends in these different places and she was interested in seeing what they were like. This was at the turn of the century. One house that we had was right next to the Catholic Cathedral in Baltimore, and I guess I was about five or so at the time - I would have been five at the turn of the century, so I'm old enough to remember the wonderful processions they had, outside, in the quadrangle, before they went in.

Q: That's right downtown in Baltimore, now.

Streeter: Yes. Absolutely. And Cardinal Gibbons was cardinal at the time, and apparently a very delightful person who was very much admired and respected by non-Catholics as well as Catholics. And he had of course a midnight mass, the night before the turn of the century, and tickets to that were vastly in demand. But my mother got a ticket, and we children were very annoyed because we were not included. We realized we were not going to see the turn of the next century, we wanted to see the turn of this century, but I think we got too sleepy and we certainly were not included.

Q: That was to be your century, anyway, that was coming up.

Streeter: That's right. Among other things, the zoo burned down that year, the Baltimore Zoo. You know, they didn't want to have all the lions and tigers burnt up, so they let them loose, and then they had quite a little time hunting down the lions and tigers before they did any damage.

Q: Any disasters?

Streeter: No, I don't think there were any disasters. Mother had a good many friends in Baltimore.

Q: Now, you were at this age - ?

Streeter: I was five, and one of the children we played with there was Revere Osler, who was the son of the famous Dr. Osler at Johns Hopkins. Revere and I took a shine to each other, got engaged, and I was thinking of moving in with him. He had cleared out the bottom drawer of his bureau, for me to put my things in.

Q: At the age of five?

Streeter: At the age of five. Unfortunately, I also looked in the drawer next to it, and Revere had a collection not only of turtles and frogs, things like that, but of snakes, and they lived in the drawer next to the one where I was to put my things. And that broke up the engagement.

I'm sorry to say that many years later, Revere was killed in the First World War. I never saw him really again after we left Baltimore. I remember that as my first love affair.

Q: Well, how long did you stay in Baltimore?

Streeter: Two different winters. And then the next winter, we went to New Orleans, and we had a very nice house in New Orleans. We enjoyed the winter there very much, and of course there was all the excitement of Mardi Gras, and I gather Mother was the belle of one of the balls there. Of course we children were not in the least neglected, but we also were not in the forefront of this activity, you understand. Children were seen but not heard, and they weren't even seen most of the time.

Q: But you had your tutor with you too?

Streeter: Yes, that's right. And here my unfortunate older brother was considered old enough to go to school, and there were only two schools in New Orleans, boys' schools, and being Southern, they were military schools. They all had to wear uniforms. One had grey uniforms for the Confederates and one had blue uniforms. My unfortunate brother was in the school with blue uniforms, which got him beaten up from time to time, on the way back and forth to school. This, you can see, was not so long after the Civil War, and feeling was still running pretty high.

However, we survived New Orleans.

Now, I think the next year, and I can't remember,

do you remember when King Edward VII was crowned? 1904, 1905?

Q: Victoria died in 1901. Edward VII was crowned in August 1902.

Streeter. Well, this was along about 1901, I guess, and this particular winter, Mother had decided she would take a trip to Japan. This was something rather unusual in those days.

Q: A very enterprising young woman, wasn't she?

Streeter: Oh, yes. She was not about to settle down in Boston, as you can see. And I don't blame her. I think she was very smart. So she got another young girl who was a friend of hers and off they went to Japan, where they had a fine time.

Q: And the children were left?

Streeter: We were left at Montecito - in California.

Q: Near Santa Barbara.

Streeter: The feeling was, we were at least 3000 miles closer, although the Pacific was awfully long and wide, and it took quite a while to get back by boat.

However, we had a lovely time. We had a little lemon ranch there, and we loved Santa Barbara, and then of course we could go swimming whenever we wanted to.

Q: Who looked after you there?

Streeter: This same teacher who had been with us all this time. We had our lessons and we had to do them. But we had a fine time.

Then when Mother was due back, we went up to San Francisco and we met her. The reason I asked, when King Edward was crowned, was because on the same ship there were all the Indian rulers in all their robes and jewels and everything else.

Then we came back by the Canadian Pacific. So all this time, we were having a good time.

Now, when was the San Francisco Fire?

Q: 1906.

Streeter: Well, it must have been another time. We went back and forth, more or less, to California, because of Grandpa's connection with the Santa Fe.

Q: Where did you stay in San Francisco?

Streeter: Well, we didn't spend the winter. I mean we just stayed there. Visited there.

We occasionally went out on a private car. My grandfather being cagy didn't have his private car, but my uncle being spendthrift had a private car, and so, we used to occasionally go in style. Other occasions we went in less style, but we still traveled back and forth, more or less, because in those days, the Santa Fe was the big thing, known in Boston as the Atchison and known everywhere else as the Santa Fe.

Q: Topeka got in there somewhere too?

Streeter: Oh, they never counted Topeka.

So we began as children to have some sense of the size of the United States, whereas if we'd grown up in Boston, we never would have, at least until we got old enough to wander on our own.

Well, the winter after that, we spent in Ottawa, Canada, and here it was fine. I remember the cold weather. It was wonderful. First thing we had to learn was not to touch the iron fence with our bare hands because our skin came off it we did. It wasn't any great temptation anyhow because we usually had mittens on.

We lived on the same street as Sir Wilfred Laurier, and we used to meet him sometimes on the sidewalk. He was a very well mannered French gentleman, and he always took off his hat to me. So I thought he was wonderful. I've got some funny pictures, I don't know where they are now, but they're absolutely side-splitting, of my brothers and myself in these stages. But what I loved was the horses and the sleighs. We had a fine big sleigh, pair of horses, and it was an open sleigh and had a great high seat in front for the coachman, that broke the wind for the people who were sitting in the back seat, and we had musk ox robes, which hung over the back and flew out, when the horses were trotting fast.

Well, also, of course there was Government House there. Government House always had the Governor General, who in those days was always an Englishman. It was Lord Minto, at the time. Ottawa wasn't very big, and Mother got fairly well known in Ottawa. She was very well accepted at Government House, and not only was Sir Wilfred a friend of hers but also Mr. King was a friend of hers, Mackenzie King. Sir Wilfred was head of the Liberal Party and Mr. King was head of the Conservative Party.

So she had a very good time in Ottawa.

Q: Was he Prime Minister in those days?

Streeter: No, but he was the leader of the opposition. And all of this was rather over our heads, but I remember it from a child's point of view very well.

Streeter #1 - 19

Q: You might tell me at this point how your own personal education was progressing? I mean, other than traveling and learning in that fashion, how was your formal education - ?

Streeter: Well, we had lessons. Oh, we had lessons every day, my brothers and myself. And then, this was getting on to about 1905 or '06, and then Mother decided that really we ought to go back to Boston and get going to a regular school, which we did. We had been sufficiently well taught at home so that none of us had any trouble catching up with our classwork in school.

Q: What subjects had you been taught by your tutor?

Streeter: Oh, all the usual ones. English, mathematics -

Q: Any foreign language?

Streeter: No. At one stage of the game we had a French teacher that taught us French. I don't remember just what stage of the game. Mostly what I remember about her is, she never opened her window at night, because she thought the outside air was going to poison her. But she was all right. This friend of Mother's who had lived with us for so long and had taught us all was Miss Eliza Kellas, and

Streeter #1 - 20

eventually as we grew up, and this was not a situation that was needed any longer, she became head of the school in Troy, New York, the Emma Willard School, and later when it became a college she was president of the Emma Willard College.

Q: Oh, really, so she was a qualified person -

Streeter: Oh yes and very much of an influence in our childhood.

Q: Did she instill any ambitions in you?

Streeter: I don't think we were ever eaten alive with ambition. We were busy, you know, just sort of keeping up with things from day to day.

Well, where have I got us to? Back in Boston.

Q: You're coming back to Boston, for formal school.

Streeter: That's it. We did. We lived at 303 Commonwealth Avenue for three years. And while we were there, something very interesting happened, because Lord Minto who had been Governor General of Canada then became Governor General of India, and this of course was more than Mother could resist, so she went out to India, and she took a friend of hers with her there who was the daughter of the Archbishop of Ottawa; and a wonderful old character who'd been with us for many years named Jeremiah O'Donoghue, who was our coachman. So he went out to look after these two ladies in India. Of course she had a wonderful time in India. This was in the days when the British Raj was really something. And she had the entree to the Governor General and this made everything very nice.

And among other things that she did when she was in India, she rode up on pony back to the Vale of Kashmir, and this was something, because they just had little pony tracks, and then when they got to these very rough canyons and rivers, they had little bridges to go across. Of course, I always wanted to go to the Vale of Kashmir after that, and I finally, at the age of 75, got there.

Q: Quite different now.

Streeter: By plane. Very differently. I didn't have to ride in. But I remember those bridges very well, and you have to be very careful about those bridges, because they go up and down, and if you happen to put your foot down when the bridge is coming up, you lose your balance - or if you put it up when the bridge is going down, you lose your balance even worse. And of course the kids and the goats and everybody else gallops across them and doesn't mind but it took me a little while to get my balance. Didn't seem to have bothered Mother at all.

So she made quite an expedition into Kashmir. You can see, if I have an adventurous soul, I probably got most of it from Mother.

Q: You certainly got some of it. Most remarkable woman, she sounds —

Streeter: Oh, she was, in many ways.
So then eventually she came back to Boston. Then she met and fell in love with Professor Schofield of Harvard University, and they were married.

Q: What area was he in?

Streeter: He was head of the department of comparative literature at Harvard, and he was a very delightful person and we were all very fond of him. They had no children. They were married until his death which was in 1920.

Q: Was he her age, or older?

Streeter: Oh, he was about her age. So then we moved to Cambridge, and there we lived in the house that belonged to Bishop Lawrence, on Brattle Street in Cambridge, where else? On one side was the Episcopal Theological School. Back of us was the Harvard Law School dormitory, very lawless bunch. The theologians used to grow geraniums in pots on their window sill, and they were nicely behaved young men. The law students were not at all nicely behaved young men. They used to make bonfires out of any spare wood we had around and dance around it. However --

Q: How did you thrive in this atmosphere?

Streeter: Oh, I throve. And it turned out eventually, when I got married, that my husband was probably one of those law students. He lived in that hall just about that time. And on the other side of us was the Longfellow House, you see. So this was what you might call a good neighborhood.

Q: Yes, I suppose it was.

Streeter: Well, soon after this, my brothers being going off to school. They went off to St. Marks, after a few years in Cambridge.

Oh, one of the things that happened then was that my stepfather, whom we used to call "Pater", he was Canadian (but he became American and we called him Pater) became exchange professor at the University of Berlin, just before World War I, I guess about 1912 or so. And this sort of turned the family interest toward Europe.

Q: Was this a year's assignment?

Streeter: Four months, I think, a semester. So they met the Kaiser, but did not like the Kaiser very much.

Q: Did the children go along?

Streeter: No, no, we stayed home. I tell you, we didn't interfere with all these things, you see. We had our little life. They had their lives. We were not neglected, by any means, but this was a different world, very different world. I mean, nowadays everybody's children are under foot, and in general they're very well behaved. I'm astonished. They're probably much more polite than we were. They take grownups in their stride, and I think it's a very fine idea, but it's totally different.

Well, somewhere along in there, as I say, Mother and Pater went to Berlin. I think it must have been - they went to Berlin, and then a little later, he had another sabbatical, and this time they went to Paris. My two brothers went to school in Geneva at a place called the Chateau de Lancy, and I went to school just outside of Paris at the Chateau de Dieudonne. This was quite a remarkable place. It was a finishing school, largely for English girls who were going to be presented at Court. When was this? This must have been about 1911, '12 -

Q: You were what age?

Streeter: I was 15. That would have been 1910. Yes, 1910. This was earlier.

Q: You were born in 1895?

Streeter: I was 15. And this place was run by the Marquise de San Carlos de Pedrosa. The Marquise was really Irish. Her mother was Irish anyhow. But she had married the Marquis, who was a grandee of Spain, but I'm not sure how admirable a grandee he was. Anyway he was a follower of old Queen Isabella, who was exiled from Spain for carrying on in ways with which I am not thoroughly familiar, but anyhow, they moved to Paris with the Queen.

Q: She was the mother of Alfonso XIII, wasn't she?

Streeter: I daresay. But she was expelled from Spain. And of course I guess they lost most of their money. They had something like five or six children, and the Marquis didn't have any money to live on, and of course he couldn't demean himself by doing any work, and so he merely shot himself, and that got him out of the way. It left Marquise with these children and no money.

So they had this little chateau. It was not one of

the fancy chateaux at all, in this little village outside of Paris, and she, with the connections that she had in England, did have mostly English girls coming, you know, to learn a little French, a little dancing, a little painting -

Q: Kind of a finishing school.

Streeter: It was definitely a finishing school, which was all right. We had to talk French every day except Sunday. We had, on our honor, to talk French all day every day, except Sunday.

Q: Dispensation on Sunday?

Streeter: Yes. Dispensation on Sunday. And there were a few Americans. There were two Dutch girls, one of whom became a great friend of mine. I kept up with her the rest of her life. And a few, couple of Rumanians and odd ones. But it was quite an experience, and again, totally different from anything that the average person in America has. I have the Marquise's book in there, that you can see some time if you want to, to show you how different it was.

Well, the chateau had a little village around it, very simple little village, and I upset their plans very much, because I had fully expected to go to Bryn Mawr when

I got home and graduated from school. Bryn Mawr, in those days, you had to take three exams in Latin, and Latin was always rather hard for me. So I didn't dare drop Latin for a year, but it certainly wasn't worth hiring somebody to come out from Paris to give me Latin. Nobody else wanted to know Latin. Couldn't have cared less about Latin.

So they asked me if I would be willing to take my Latin studies under Monsieur le Curé of the village?

Well, M. le Curé was a good village type. I met him one day coming back from the fields in his cassock with his pitchfork over his arm. He'd been out tilling his field. But he knew his Latin, and he knew his French, and he had a wonderful scroll writing, you know.

Q: Palmer type, but European.

Streeter: Yes. But he had no English. And I had to deal with Cicero and the Cataline Orations that winter, very full work.

Q: Yes, I thought so too.

Streeter: Well, anyhow, there were four of them, and my French was not good enough or my Latin to translate first from Latin into French. So I translated from Latin into

English and then from English into French. You know, this was quite a job. Mostly I memorized it. But I did it all in copybooks, and M. le Curé corrected it conscientiously and carefully, and his French was very good and his Latin was very good, and it gave me a sound basis in Latin, for whatever good that might have done me. What it really did, I think, was, you know, to teach me discipline, the discipline of study.

Q: Well, it certainly was an intellectual exercise, too.

Streeter: Well, of sorts. That was the first semester. That was the autumn semester, which made it nice to be in the country. Then the winter semester, they moved into Paris, into a nice house in Paris, and then —

Q: And your stepfather was teaching in Paris?

Streeter: Yes, he was giving some courses at the Sorbonne. Then that spring was the time when King George V was crowned. Mother and Pater, having friends in England, went over for the Coronation. And at that time, we had Jerry O'Donoghue's son. He was the Irish coachman who'd gone with Mother to India, and his son went over as our chauffeur, to Paris. So while Mother and Pater were in England at the Coronation for a couple of weeks, my brothers were getting out of school, I was getting out of school, so we went over to Geneva. Joe took us over. I collected the boys, and on one trip, because we used to have him drive us around the countryside, we had found a very interesting place, in the Vosges, I guess, not in the Alps, but on the way to the Swiss border, a little valley in the mountains, and at this time you see, the Catholics, the orders, had been kicked out and their property confiscated by the state, so this was a Carthusian Monastery. They're the silent ones, you know, not allowed to talk. And the owner of it was a woman. It had descended to this lone woman, and she offered to give it to the church if she could become a Carthusian, so they allowed her to become a Carthusian, and she built this church in the middle of the quadrangle of the chateau. It was on one side and then there were all the cells around the other three sides. Of course it wasn't used for some time after it was confiscated, and then an enterprising restorateur from Lyons, I think, had come up there and was making a summer hotel out of it.

The way these cells were arranged, a door would open up onto the corridor, but one side of the little cell was a blank wall, the other side had a door and a window opening into a garden but facing three blank walls, you see, the blank wall of the corridor, the blank wall of the back of the next cell, and the outside wall. So you had your own little house and your own little garden. And as we did not have to go to church every hour on the hour, we had a pleasant time, my brothers and I, and we explored the countryside round about. As I remember, it was the cherry season, so we had some cherries.

Q: Red cherries.

Streeter: Yes. So our time passed very pleasantly while Mother and Pater were over at the Coronation.

Then after that, I guess my brothers had to go back to school, but I didn't go in the spring term, and we went up to Norway and Denmark and Sweden, and I went up with Mother and Pater. So I really was seeing quite a lot of the world.

Then we came back to Boston and I finished school. The boys graduated. My older brother went to Harvard. My younger brother was about to go.

Well, then I came out. Now, life in Boston in those days was BC - before coming out, and after coming out.

Q: And the coming out age was?

Streeter: Eighteen. Coming out was a big event and it took a whole year. So maybe that's another chapter.

Q: Yes.

Interview With Ruth Cheney Streeter (Mrs. Thomas W. Streeter)
At her home, Morristown, New Jersey
May 21, 1979
By John T. Mason, Jr.

Q: We should begin this chapter today, Mrs. Streeter, by saying something about the immediate members of your family. You haven't said a great deal heretofore.

Mrs. Streeter: I will be very glad to say something about that, because we were actually a very close family. Naturally, my father having died when I was a baby, my mother was the stronger influence in my life for a long time.

Q: And a tremendously strong person, too.

Mrs. Streeter: She was.

Q: Which you have indicated.

Mrs. Streeter: Yes, and a very interesting person, and she had a very annoying way of being right practically all the time. I did not always appreciate it when I was young, but I appreciated it later.

She remarried when I was about, I think, thirteen, and we were all very fond of our stepfather, who was a professor at Harvard, and a very kind and gentle and knowledgeable and understanding sort of a person. It must have been quite a problem to him, I think, coming into a family of teenagers. But he adapted very well. He did not attempt to discipline us, which would probably have caused a revolution. But he was somebody that we used to talk to quite often when we had things on our minds, and he was always willing to listen, and rather tolerant and understanding of our adolescent ideas.

Q: Well, of course, he'd been teaching students for some time, hadn't he?

Streeter: Yes. Oh, yes. He had. He was head of the department of comparative literature at Harvard, and he was master of Claverly Hall, where he of course had rooms along with the students. I think he must have been an understanding and reasonably tolerant master, because they all seemed to like him too.

He and my mother did not have any children. Later on, after my marriage, he was in poor health about the time that our second son was born, and did eventually die, and we named our second son after him, Henry Schofield Streeter. We managed to get up from New York with the baby a few weeks before Pater died. We thought this was the best tribute that we could pay to him, and show him how much we really cared about him.

My mother spent a very active and interesting life in many respects. That is a whole story by itself, and I'd probably better not go into it at length now, but she had first built this lovely house in Peterborough, New Hampshire after my father's death, and then she built a little stone church, sort of early English church, in the town of Peterborough. The architect was Ralph Adams Cram, and it is really a beautiful church of its type and time. It had lovely glass in it, and many very beautiful memorials, and is quite widely known.

In order to do that, she had really studied a great deal about church architecture, and when we were in Europe, any time, we went to every cathedral there was, within reach. And that succeeded in giving us a little background about ecclesiastical architecture also.

Later on, after her children began to get married and have children of their own, she took up an interest in nursery school, which was then a very new idea, and started one in Peterborough.

We looked with mixed ideas upon that, because we thought that it was possibly an indication that we were not bringing up our children as well as we should. But we did get some very good ideas from the school that she had up there.

Q: You were sensitive about it.

Streeter: We were not sure just what her motives were!

She also took an active part in politics, and among other things was an Elector, a member of the Electoral College when President Coolidge was elected. She then took a great interest in many public works in New Hampshire, both in the wars and also in peace time, and eventually was given an honorary MA from the University of New Hampshire.

And all this time, she continued to be a very interesting and attactive hostess. She had all the social graces and a great many friends.

I think that I was not quite what my mother expected me to be, because after a year abroad and a great coming out year, I was supposed to be a "jeune fille", and I don't suppose anybody nowadays knows what a "jeune fille" used to be expected to be. But she was sugar and sweet and everything nice. And I was given certainly all of the opportunities.

Having however grown up between two brothers, I had a tomboy streak, I'm afraid, which lay underneath the arts and graces which I had been taught, and which occasionally broke out. My two brothers and I were very close to each other because of our ages, and also because during our growing up years we had not been to school. We had traveled around, and we had had a teacher at home. This teacher was a very interesting person. Her name was Miss Eliza Kellas, and after she had brought us up, she took some extra courses at Radcliffe, the winter that we lived in Cambridge, and became the head of the Emma Willard School in Troy, New York, and later when it became a college, she was president of the Emma Willard College.

Q: You were surrounded by unusual women, were you not?

Streeter: Oh, but definitely. However, I seemed to hold my own pretty well in those days.

Well, all of this background, of course, was sort of absorbed, without perhaps my knowing that it was being absorbed.

My two brothers were quite different. My older brother was a good student. He had poor eyesight, but that didn't interfere with his studies, and he was a reliable type. After we were all in college and all on allowances, with which we were supposed to pay our own way - we always ran out before the quarter was up, my younger brother and I did, and we always had to borrow from my older brother.

Q: But he always had it.

Streeter: He always had the money and we always repaid him, but he seemed to be able to make it last three months, and we didn't.

My younger brother was the athletic type and sort of easy going. If I ever had a date with either one of them, and one was fifteen minutes late, if it was my older brother I always waited, because I knew he'd just been delayed, he would show up. If it was my younger brother, I didn't wait more than fifteen minutes. I knew he'd forgotten it.

Q: And that distinguishes between the two.

Streeter: Yes. Sure. We were very close to each other, as I say, because we'd all grown up - and for many many years, all disputes were amicably settled by a vote of 2 to 1. And this, I think, is probably unusual.

Q: This was a common agreement that you arrived at.

Streeter: All settled. No great hair pullings or anything like that.

Q: What role did Miss Kellas have to play in that?

Streeter: Well, she was in the background. This was

between the three of us.

Q: Yes, but in inculcating that idea.

Streeter: Oh, I don't think so. I think we worked that out by ourselves. But she taught us, and she was a good strong character, and we were not encouraged in sloppy ways by anybody. I think this was very fine.

Actually, one of the things that impresses me, as I look around the world at the present time, and the upbringing of the young, is, how all the influences in our youth managed to get together. The church, the home, and the school all taught us one thing, and what they taught us was, "No one can tell what the future may bring, of joy or sorrow, of good things or bad things, but what you bring to meet the future, that is within your power."

Now, nobody has ever told a psychiatrist. It's a totally different approach to life. And I'm rather glad that we were taught that. And we had no way not to believe it, because everybody told us the same thing.

Q: It was the prevailing attitude.

Streeter: It was the prevailing attitude.

Q: Did you see, as you grew older and had children of

your own, did you see any change taking place, say, through the agency of the nursery school and that sort of thing?

Streeter: Never sent them to nursery school.

Q: But your mother set one up.

Streeter: Oh yes, but we didn't go to it. She set it up in the village of Peterborough.

Q: Yes, but did you discern a different idea beginning to develop in that area?

Streeter: Yes, but we didn't pay very much attention to it.

Q: Was your mother's nursery school being inspected by -

Streeter: - some nursery school authorities, and they were duly impressed. It was a well known school. And finally, they said, "But Mrs. Schofield, what do you do with the problem of negativism?"

And Mother smiled sweetly at them and said, "We do not have any problem of negativism." I'm sure they didn't!

Mother sometimes had a problem of negativism with us, but she dealt with it quite effectively. And there were no ill feelings left afterwards, either.

So, I'm trying simply to show that we had really a very happy childhood, and I think a well-rounded childhood, in spite of it being somewhat different from the average bringing up. Especially in the matter of schooling.

Q: I might ask you at this point, what role the church did play in your development?

Streeter: Oh, we got taken to church quite regularly. And we were duly confirmed when the time came to be confirmed, and all of us were Episcopalians, but how good we are or not, I don't know.

I think that we had a foundation of church upbringing which I think is largely a matter of custom, but also a matter of acceptance of the general content of religion. This, I don't want to get into at great length, but it has always seemed to me that people needed religion, and maybe they looked upon it more or less as an allegory, but at least it was a good allegory. And a helpful one.

Returning now to more mundane things - how far have we actually gotten in this history?

Q: We're going to deal with the period when you returned, with the family, from abroad, after having spent some time there and being in school in France.

Streeter: Yes. By this time, I think I had two more years in school in Boston, and then I was eighteen, and I was ready to come out.

Q: What Kkind of school did you attend in Boston?

Streeter: Oh, I went to Miss May's School in Boston. This was a day school. It was the one I'd been to, all the time that I was back in Boston. It went from nine to one. We had twenty minutes recess, in which we usually had an apple, and we walked to school and we walked home from school, about a mile, except some days when it was very bad weather and the chauffeur picked me up.

But we had no afternoon school. None of this business of not being home till 4 o'clock or anything. And no buses, of course. We went to school in the morning - you brought your homework home with you. If you wanted piano lessons or riding lessons or whatever else you wanted, and your family was able to afford it, that was provided by them in the afternoons. It was no part of your school lessons. And I think that there is something to be said for that arrangement, although it's nowadays become so different, and so many mothers especially are working that it's impractical to go back to it.

By the time I came out, which was in the fall of 1913, my older brother was at Harvard. My younger brother was still at St. Mark's School, where he became captain of the football team his last year. And I was in between.

Coming out in Boston in those days was an <u>event</u>. Looking back on it, it seems out of this world. In the first place, there was no income tax until 1913. People could afford to give big parties and they did. It was the last year that that sort of thing happened for a long time, because in the summer of 1914 of course the war started in Europe. But the winter of '13 - '14 was a time when girls really did COME OUT, and of course, with Harvard boys across the river, there were plenty of escorts for you.

Q: How many girls on the average came out in Boston in a given season?

Streeter: In those years, I would say, about fifty.

Q: Who was the mentor who determined this?

Streeter: Oh yes, there were the Sewing Circles. The Sewing Circles, not the Junior League, in those days. There was a Sewing Circle for each year, and last year's Sewing Circle selected the first ten of the new year. They selected the next twenty-five. I was about down in the middle. I was in the next twenty-five. And then those thirty-five selected the next few, which were about fifteen.

Q: And the eligibility was determined by what?

Streeter: By them.

Q: I know, but what did they use as a yardstick, so to speak?

Streeter: Well, what a question to ask me! What do you use as yardsticks for that sort of thing?

Q: What determined eligibility?

Streeter: Well, family, mostly. And personal quality. And to a certain extent, wealth. They all belonged to more or less a certain group of grownups in Boston. They were the children of certain groups of grownups in Boston. And there had been one, ever since the Civil War, each year. I still belong to the 1913 Sewing Circle, what is left of it. I haven't had an invitation to a meeting for quite a while. I don't believe there are many of us left.

Q: Was there much sewing done in the Sewing Circle?

Streeter: In my day, there was no sewing done. But we had a certain interest in how the other half lived. I think our exposure was sort of cosmetic, to how the other half lived, but we would go down and work in a settlement or work in a hospital, or that sort of thing. But our main occupation was a luncheon. I can't remember whether it was weekly. I can't believe it was, although it might have been. It might have been monthly. These luncheons were given by some of us for the rest of us, and the hostess was very carefully told what she could give, because some of the members of course had a great deal of money and some didn't have so much money, so it was limited to two dishes, an entree and a dessert, plus cocoa or tea. Don't think we were expected to have coffee in those days. Certainly nothing stronger.

Q: Not even wine at the table?

Streeter: Oh, no. Of course by this time we knew all about alcohol because we went to parties. But not Sewing Circle parties. In fact, we learned quite a lot about alcohol from the Harvard boys, who were indispensable, of course, to dances.

This Sewing Circle business later developed into the Junior League, but not until after World War I. A New York group started the Junior League, and then they sold the idea to a number of other cities, who all had their own individual groups similar to the Sewing Circles in Boston, and they absorbed the Sewing Circles. And the Junior League, as people know by this time, I'm sure, is an enormously influential organization. It's not very noisy about what it does, but it does an awful lot of good. And they are really serious about the work that they do. In fact the requirements, the working requirements are very very stiff, I think.

When I eventually came out here to Morristown, I had been transferred from the Boston League to the New York League, and to my horror, I discovered that the same type of girls in Morristown were all commuting into New York to work in New York settlement houses and hospitals, when we had similar things right here in Morristown and similar problems.

And I talked with some of the girls out here and said, "Why don't you say, Morristown will do this type of thing? Would you be interested in having a Junior League in Morristown?"

And a number of them said they would be. There were two others girls here at that time who like myself belonged to the New York Junior League, and they were willing to sponsor a new one out here.

About that time, the New York League was being snowed under by members, because they included Westchester, Connecticut, New Jersey shore. They had too many people, and they were willing to back up the formation of new Leagues, and I managed to talk myself onto that committee, and that was a help.

Q: Well, the person who proposes it is usually put in charge of it.

Streeter: So that has grown. It's now been active here in Morristown for over fifty years. Does an enormous amount of good. And it also is a great benefit to the members, because so many have not any real roots anywhere. Their parents have been moved around or their jobs have moved them around. And when they come to a new community, they have this group at once which is congenial and with whom they can identify.

So every year they have what are called provisional members, and they take them around and give them what we used to call in the military service a briefing, which is never at all brief. It lasts a good many weeks with this Junior League.

Q: But actually briefing them by taking them to the various projects, and - ?

Streeter: Yes. And they almost always have me come and say a few words to them about how the Junior League started.

Well, that was the more or less serious side of coming out. But it was a curious sort of tribal rite, as I look back upon it. It was, in fact, your parents announcing to your particular world that they now had a marriageable daughter. And at the moment, I was not particularly interested in marriage, because I wanted to go to college for a couple of years anyhow. But nevertheless, I went through the usual routine, and it was enjoyable. It was also, I suppose, quite useful, as far as learning your way around in certain circles was concerned. Up to that time, you'd been a school girl.

I think anybody who came out in Boston, or almost any one of these similar cities, could be transplanted anywhere and not feel lost. You knew how to conduct yourself; if you were married and moved to Texas or somewhere else, you didn't feel completely at sea. It was a long and rather elaborate way of teaching you those things, but on the whole I think it worked.

Oh, my mother and stepfather gave me a big ball in the Hotel Somerset. This was quite an affair. We had two orchestras, and a large number of people, and it really was done in style.

Then the other great thing that happened that winter was a visit we made to Ottawa. As you would know from the previous chapter in this oral history, we had spent a winter in Ottawa, and mother had friends among the people there, and my stepfather was Canadian, and so he had connections there too, and this was now the winter of 1914.

The Governor-General in those days was sent out by England to Canada, and was an Englishman, not a Canadian.

This particular Governor-General was the Duke of Devonshire, and their daughter was the Princess Patricia, who later became Princess Pat, the patron saint of the Canadian regiments in Europe.

But at this time the war was not even in the offing to us and the Governor-General had the equivalent of a presentation at court. In Ottawa it was held in the Senate room of the House of Parliament, and Mother and Pater managed to get me on the list. So we went up there.

Q: And you were quite willing?

Streeter: Oh yes, I was, you know, sort of adventurous. As I've told you, and I was quite willing. So we went up there, and it was quite impressive. The Duke sat on a throne, no less, and his wife the Duchess and the Princess Patricia sat on chairs, but below the dias.

Then of course there was a row of officers, all in their dress uniforms. By this time, I'd met some. That was not helpful, because out of the side of their mouths they'd make remarks to you as you walked up the hall between two rows of them.

Those of us that were being presented, we wore evening dress, but we had three white feathers and a white veil, and their favorite remark was, "Oh dear, your feathers have got crooked."

Anything that was inclined to make you wonder if you were going to fall down when it came your time to curtsey.

But usually you managed to keep your self possession, and you got up to the head of the line, and you duly curtseyed to the —

Q: — and you'd done some practicing.

Streeter: Oh, yes, you certainly had done practicing. You made your curtsey to the Duke.

I was fascinated by him, because I was sure, if he'd bowed his head each time he'd have gotten an awful stiff neck the next morning. There were, oh, I don't know how many of us. A hundred or more of us.

And then, he had it all arranged so that he bowed from the hips, just leaned forward from the hips.

I was fascinated. And then of course you had to sidle off. You couldn't turn your back on the representative of royalty, so you sidled out, after you had made your curtsey, and scuttled upstairs to the gallery, where you then went back and watched and made comments on all the people that made their curtseys after you.

Q: Were they largely Canadian girls?

Streeter: Yes, mostly. I don't know, I don't suppose they

have this any more, because the Governor Generals are of course Canadians now, and I think much of this pomp and circumstance has gone the way of a great deal of other pomp and circumstance. But it was a definite experience, in those days.

Q: And then I suppose there was a ball there?

Streeter: Oh, yes.

Q: Or a series of balls.

Streeter: Well, as I remember it, of course I think there was dancing afterwards. I'm not perfectly certain because I'm not perfectly certain that the accommodations lent themselves to it. I don't remember that part of it. But also, there were various dinners and things given for us. As I told you, Mother had made good friends in Ottawa the winter that we were all up there, and had been to Government House quite often and knew Lord and Lady Minto quite well. So this all continued to be of the pattern of good will in Ottawa. This is the first time I had been really to a formal dinner. This is the time I learned about "trifles." I'd never had a trifle before in my life. When the table was cleared, after the dessert, I thought of course we'd get up and go to the next room pretty soon. But not at all.

Along came the trifle. And I was charmed by the trifles.

Q: And then there was a division of the men and women?

Streeter: Oh, yes. Oh, yes. A very good idea, too.

Then I came back to Boston, and by that time, the Boston season was pretty well over. But we had another very fine party down at New Haven for the Harvard-Yale Boat Race, a house party down there, and Mother wangled a house somehow or other. So we enjoyed that very much.

Then in the summer, we relaxed a little bit.

Q: How many parties would you say that you were involved in, in the year that you were coming out?

Streeter: Oh, good gracious. Dances, I suppose maybe twenty. And dinner dances, a good many of them were, and before a dance, you would have a dinner. Somebody gave a dinner. And luncheons. All kinds of things. You didn't do much of anything else.

Q: You didn't have time to do anything else.

Streeter: You didn't have time to do anything, or energy, to do very much else.

Q: And I suppose you made frequent trips to the dressmaker.

Streeter: Yes. Yes, that was essential, too.

Q: Did you have a new outfit for every ball?

Streeter: No, no. Of course you didn't. You couldn't go that far. But it was, as I look back upon it, it was extreme in Boston, in those days, and probably in a number of other cities, Baltimore, for instance. After the war, World War I, I mean, that whole business to some extent changed. Of course, by that time we were in New York, and usually two or three girls' families would get together and give a dinner dance or something. There weren't so many balls, large scale balls. And then of course after World War II, it vanished almost entirely. You might have a coming out tea or something. You didn't go through all this elaborate stage setting.

At that time, of course, after the spring of 1914, the next thing that happened was World War I, which broke out in August of 1914.

Q: "The Guns of August."

Streeter: Yes, absolutely. And of course, at that time we had no idea that America would be in it. I remember the great excitement we had in our family, "I hope such and such a country isn't going to lie down under this," a regular rah rah feeling about this war, you know, and absolutely no understanding of what a war would be like.

Then we had the calm before the storm for two years. And then in 1917, of course, we were in it ourselves.

That is a whole other period. I think the growing up period lasted through the spring of '14, as far as I was concerned. Then I began to think of going to college, and that is a whole other story.

Q: The popular concept of the upper strata in Boston of course is the Boston Brahmin. Now, this was a whole part of your picture, was it not?

Streeter: Well, it was a part of the picture, but I certainly never was a Boston Brahmin.

I mean, I knew the Cabots and the Lowells, but I didn't belong to that particular group. We were all in the same Sewing Circle. We went to the same parties and all that. My grandfather, as I think I told you, started life as a stage coach driver. But if you go back far enough in the Lowells, you know, they started with textile people and all that. So, just where your blue blood comes in, in Boston - is an open question.

Q: And just what is "blue blood"?

Streeter: And just what is a Brahmin? A good many became what you might call Brahmins, but if you went back for two generations, they weren't necessarily so.

Q: Well, now we come to a juncture in your life when you determined to go off to college. You might say something about the prevailing attitude in Boston at that time about young women going off to college, the percentage who did, from your circle? That sort of thing.

Streeter: Yes. Some, of course, went to college right near Boston, such as Radcliffe and Wellesley. I was by that time feeling my oats a little bit, and I didn't want to go to college so close to Boston. I wanted to go to some place where, you know, nobody ever heard of me and my family before, and try standing on my own feet.

Q: Of course your mother had been at Wellesley.

Streeter: My mother had been at Wellesley, and I think Wellesley is a fine college. But I also think Bryn Mawr is a fine college, and that is where I decided I'd like to go.

Q: What induced you to Bryn Mawr? I mean, what induced

you to think in terms of Bryn Mawr?

Streeter: Well, the other colleges wouldn't agree, but I think it was rather generally considered to be the best, the hardest and the best. Anyhow, I liked the idea.

Of people in my Sewing Circle, my roommate went to Bryn Mawr too. She'd been a classmate at Miss May's. There were maybe three others at Bryn Mawr and possibly some more, but there were certainly less than ten, I would say, out of the fifty in my Sewing Circle who went to college. And I myself did not go to college with the idea of staying four years and getting a job. This being more or less also my mother's influence, I think, because that was her idea. She'd only been two years to Wellesley. And most girls with my background expected to get married and have their husbands support them and their family, and did not particularly expect to get jobs. A few wanted to be doctors or perhaps teachers or some one of the professions. But at that time, it was rather unusual to go to college, and even in Boston it was regarded as being sort of a bluestocking - and frowned upon by the young men that we knew, mostly. Oh, yes. They didn't particularly care for a brainy gal for a wife.

Q: That attitude somewhat prevails today, I think.

Streeter: Well, I wouldn't know. I would have thought it would have changed some in sixty years, but maybe not.

In any case, my general attitude toward life was that I would like to go to college for a couple of years, and find out what it was like to stand on my own feet, and I was sure it would be interesting, and then, probably, get married and settle down. I was definitely not interested in getting married before I went to college.

Q: You hadn't any young man in mind, anyway.

Streeter: No particular one, no. So, that was more or less my frame of mind at that time.

Q: And so you went off to Bryn Mawr in 1914?

Streeter: In the fall of 1914. And for the first two years at college, the war in Europe was quite shadowy to us. This is partly because it was shadowy to most Americans. We had no idea of getting into it for some time. It was also probably especially shadowy for people at college, because they were more or less detached from what was going on in the world, and concentrating on their own particular studies and efforts. In any case, it had no particular effect on me, until after I'd left college and things began to get worse, in the fall of '16 and the spring of '17.

Q: Can you give me a picture of life in a women's college in the year 1914?

Streeter: Yes. I think there was nothing about it that isn't generally known. Bryn Mawr in those days of course was strictly a women's college. It was sort of an avant garde women's college, so considered in those days. M. Carey Thomas was the president, and oh my, she was a great character. She had made Bryn Mawr what it was. She came of a Quaker family. She had gotten her Ph.D. in Germany because she couldn't get one in this country. She was quite certain that education was the answer to all evil. I don't know if she was ever persuaded otherwise. It just seemed to me a little doubtful that it was such a sweeping cure for all evil, but -

Q: - and now from your present perspective, you still don't think so?

Streeter: I'm not entirely convinced, no. But in those days at Bryn Mawr, you certainly studied. And I think if you go to college, by gum, you should study.

I do not in the least hold with sending people to college and having them take survey courses and get a lot of credits for things that don't amount to anything. I'm vastly interested to see that Harvard, after thirty years of general education, is now going back to the basics. We never got away from the basics. In fact, in order to graduate, you must have had one year of Latin or one year of Greek, after you went there. You also had to take an examination, oral examination in French, and German I think, in your senior year or before your senior year. And then you had certain special classes that you had to take, special courses. Since I went with the idea of not staying for four years. I did not take all those required courses. I browsed. I thought that would be more interesting.

There was one thing that I didn't browse in - again, more or less my mother's influence, and that shows how far ahead of her time Mother was. She was interested in South America. She said, "I think the future of North America lies in its ties with South America even more than with Europe or the Orient."

So she said, "Why don't you learn Spanish?" So instead of taking English, which was a required course for two years five days a week, I took Spanish for a required course five days a week. This was certainly sort of a waste of time, because you don't learn a foreign language in the grammar and translation business the way we did in those days. I think now they teach it more verbally and by records and things like that.

Q: The two together makes a very fine combination.

Streeter: Yes. Of course, if you had some Latin and some French, Spanish wasn't going to be awfully hard for you. But I never became fluent in it, and of course when I didn't use it, I lost it almost entirely.

However, I took a lot of other things, mostly of course the beginning courses in them, because I was only there freshman and sophomore years. They had one good course which was economics one semester and politics the other semester. I got an A in politics. What that means I wouldn't know except that it was sort of a snap course.

Q: Maybe it shows an aptitude.

Streeter: Well, I later went more or less into politics, though not necessarily because of that.

They had another one which was a semester each of philosophy and psychology, and those were interesting. Then I took a very interesting one in history of art, which was something I knew very little about and wanted to know more about. And I took biology, and that I was really interested in. If I had ever thought of going into a profession, what I would have liked to have gone into would have been medicine, but I'm not sure I had the brains ever to have gone into that. But I was fascinated with biology and I also got an A in that, which was much harder to get than the A in politics. For the rest —

Q: — and in the laboratory, too, wasn't it?

Streeter: Oh, sure. For the rest, I think, I had a good average. You see, I had not been taking just the things that were easy or snap courses, with the exception of politics, or the things I was good at, at all. History of art I was no good at, and philosophy and psychology, not particularly good at, especially philosophy.

So, I think my average was about 82, which was pretty good at Bryn Mawr. If I could have kept it up I would have been in the first ten of my class. But I'm not sure if I could have kept it up, if I'd had to take the required courses. So, you know, I did put my mind considerably on my lessons. But I also did a lot of other things.

Q: What were some of the other things?

Streeter: Well, first thing, I became vice president of the freshman class. The president was selected by the president of the sophomore class, the previous sophomore class from entering freshmen and made temporary president for about six weeks so that the freshmen would have some form of organization when they first arrived. Then they had a class meeting to elect their own officers, because by that time they'd gotten a little acquainted with each other.

The freshman president was Bessie Downs of Philadelphia,

who later married Roland Evans, the father of the columnist. I was vice president. Bessie left at the end of the freshman year and I became president sophomore year.

Q: How large were the classes?

Streeter: Our class was 100 when it went in, and I think it graduated 70 to 75. Quite a good many left for one reason or another before graduation.

Q: So you were early displaying leadership qualities.

Streeter: Well, I suppose something of the sort. I was feeling my oats, mostly. I tried everything. On the theory that that would help me find out what I was good at and what I wasn't good at.

Now, this is something which bothered me for years; about my grandchildren's age; my own children, I would say, took college pretty seriously. Some of my grandchildren did not. And at that time, and less now but certainly during the sixties or seventies, children went to college and they came out of college no more knowledgeable about themselves than they went in, after four years. They came out. They didn't know what they were good at. They didn't know what they wanted to do. And they wasted a good deal of time in college, and I think that was pretty silly.

Nowadays their parents can't stand the expense of sending them to college unless they're going to do something about it. You can't just park them there and let them have a good time. Of course, the Vietnam War made college a refuge, which was the worst mistake in the whole Vietnam War. They never should have been a refuge and they were not a refuge in World War II. If you got excused to go to college, it was because you were expected to be an officer when you came out, and that was a prerequisite to go, to be excused from the draft. But during Vietnam they just went and sheltered in the colleges. Bad for the colleges, bad for them, bad for the country.

Q: Going back to an idea you expressed about your efforts while in college, it was to determine what you were good at and what you couldn't do, what your real aptitudes were.

Now, what caused you to be able to do that, in contrast with the youngsters of today?

Streeter: The bringing up I told you about.

Q: The bringing up.

Streeter: Which said, what you do to meet the future depends on you. And that's exactly what has been missing, at times, in a great many families nowadays.

One thing I was not good at was water polo. I did pretty well on the shallow end of the tank, where I could keep one foot on the floor, I was goalie, but I didn't do so well in the deep end of the tank.

Q: Back to ground —

Streeter: That's right. So I belonged to a lot of things. I was in the Christian Association. I was head of the Employment Bureau one year.

Q: Head of the Employment Bureau?

Streeter: Well, I know, but we didn't have much to employ. For instance, we would produce umpires for field hockey teams, and if nobody else could be produced, I had to be umpire myself. It was a very sketchy employment. And then people took notes for people who had been sick and couldn't attend their classes. You see. It was that small thing. You couldn't really earn enough money to be anything except spending money.

Q: Were many of the girls involved in earning anything to supplement their —

Streeter: It didn't supplement it enough to be worth trying

Streeter #2 - 63

to do — not real jobs with real pay, just spending money.

Q: Were there any scholarships available?

Streeter: Oh, yes. There have always been those.

So, as I say, I tried anything that I saw that looked interesting, and I certainly found some things I was no good at.

I did seem to have some relation to my classmates, which was mutually satisfactory, I suppose, as you will see later on.

Anyhow, I did spend these two years there. I was always very appreciative of what Bryn Mawr had done for me, the opportunity it had given me to expand, and for some twenty-five years I was a very strong Bryn Mawrter, though I had not graduated.

Q: Let me ask you, was there any temptation, during those two years while you were there, to lift your sights, change your sights and decide to go on and finish four years?

Streeter: Not especially. As I said a little earlier, if I had wanted to do anything, I would have liked to go into medicine, but outside of getting an A in freshman biology, I had no particular reason to suppose I'd be capable of doing it. And it would have been a very long hard preparation, and I didn't have that much ambition. So, I never objected at all to just going two years.

Q: How closely did your mother look after you there at Bryn Mawr?

Streeter: Not at all, to speak of.

Q: She didn't?

Streeter: I was on an allowance. She looked after me in the summer vacations and all that, but I was on my allowance as I told you. I didn't always stay on it without help from my elder brother, but –

Q: Was he still available for borrowing?

Streeter: Oh, yes. He was at Harvard.

Q: And he could still –

Streeter: Oh, yes, he could.

Q: You went to him rather than to your mother.

Streeter: Yes. Oh, yes. As I say, Mother put us up during

vacations, you see. Really we got a quarterly allowance but some quarters we spent more than other quarters. Of course we sponged on the family during holidays.

Q: And where were the holidays spent, largely in Peterborough?

Streeter: Yes. The summer holiday would be in Peterborough.

Well, by the time I left college, it was the spring of 1916, and of course, when you were out of college in the spring of '16, you became much more conscious of what was going on in Europe. And I think you can say that this time ended the carefree period of my life, and I think probably of all my contemporaries" lives too.

Q: It was a watershed time.

Streeter: A watershed time. We can go into that part of my existence later. If you would like, we can now go on with my connections with Bryn Mawr.

Q: I wish you would, yes, and make that a chapter.

Streeter: Well, as I say, I was a very enthusiastic Bryn Mawrter and I did all kinds of odd jobs that the Alumnae Association gave me. But the main thing was that when our class graduated in 1918, they elected as their permanent

Streeter #2 - 66

president a girl whose father was an Army officer. And by '18 of course, by '19 anyhow, the war was over. Germany was being occupied. She spent a year with him in Germany, and then he was transferred to Hawaii. So she felt that as an Army brat, she never could tell where she was going to be, and that she ought to resign as president. So a mail ballot was held, and I was elected president.

Q: Even though you hadn't been there for two years?

Streeter: Hadn't been there for three years, by that time. And had never graduated.

Q: My, this is a commentary on leadership.

Streeter: Well, I was very pleased of course, and did my best. As a matter of fact, I was president for 39 years. And then after our 40th anniversary, I figured it was time somebody else became president, and retired, and the gal who had been president first took over. Because what had happened was that within a year, she went back to Bryn Mawr, got a job at Bryn Mawr, married the professor of chemistry and stayed there the rest of her life! I tried to get the Presidency back on her shoulders when I discovered that; but she wouldn't take it until after our 40th reunion in 1958.

Q: How exceedingly interesting.

Streeter: It was a funny combination of events.

Well, let me see. Meanwhile, the big event was the 50th anniversary of the college.

Q: The 50th anniversary of the college itself would fall in 1935.

Streeter: In 1935, and I remember distinctly marching in the academic procession, because it was rather impressive, and I was the only person in it, although I wore a cap and gown, who had no hood!

Q: No degree.

Streeter: This you may consider distinction of a sort, but I'm not sure whether it was the right sort or not. Anyway, I was offered a hood for the occasion. I turned it down. I said, "No, I didn't earn it, won't wear it."

Now we have to make quite a great leap forward in time, because, the time we've just been discussing, when I was at Bryn Mawr, was on the eve of World War I; and twenty-five years afterwards, we were in World War II. And when we come to that later, we will talk about my connection with World War II.

Q: Yes, your military involvement.

Streeter: And how I went to the Marine Corps.

This period became rather a curious relationship between Bryn Mawr and myself. I had, among other things, when I first went in the Marine Corps, to make a tour of the country, mostly visiting women's colleges or coeducational colleges for recruiting. I did not at first realize, although I later came to do so, that although I always had a courteous reception, it was slightly cool. Then I began to notice that the women's colleges were having a real conflict of interest, they were never quite square enough to face, between losing their undergraduates and maintaining the colleges. Alumnae of all the women's colleges went into the armed forces, quantities of them, and the colleges had no objection to that, of course, because they were out. But the colleges were anxious, and they did not get behind the armed forces as far as the undergraduates were concerned because they didn't want to lose them.

Now, this is quite understandable. The undergraduates were their source of income. The tuitions were their source of income. But the colleges never admitted it. I think they never admitted it even to themselves.

They need not have been quite so worried about it, because the age limits for women were twenty. Nobody under twenty. And if you were twenty years old you could certainly have had two years of college and possibly three. So it was not quite the threat to them that I think they were inclined to feel it was.

Eventually, in fact with in a year of the time that the Marine Corps Women's Reserve was formed, the qualifications were changed, and to be an officer, and of course most girls in college would expect to be officers, they had to have a college degree.

Now, it was fortunate for me that in the beginning the qualification was two years of college plus additional work experience, so I qualified at that time. But it was promptly changed, because they got so many applications from college graduates that they felt it was a good thing to make that a regular qualification for officers.

We did, however, draw many of them for enlisted women, and looking back over the records the other day, I was surprised again at how many women with some college education did go in as enlisted women.

Now, the statistics that I was reading the other day show that out of some 23,145 women, which would include more than the thousand officers as well as the 13,000 women, because of course we had a turnover to some extent in the course of three years war, there were 4,478 with some college education, between one and four years.

Q: As enlisted personnel.

Streeter: No, out of the whole –

Q: – the total?

Streeter: – including the officers. Now, that's quite a lot. And I think most of them were one or two year women who went in as enlisted personnel.

The reason for that, and it shows that the individual women had more appreciation I think of the situation than the colleges did – they didn't want to wait to be officers. This was true of the men. A great many college men didn't wait to be officers. They went in as enlisted.

These women probably had someone in their family, their fathers, their brothers, their boy friends, who had enlisted. And they wanted to enlist too. Also, I think they had a more accurate feeling about the condition of this country at that time than the colleges did. We were being licked and I don't think the colleges ever admitted that. Their point was that it would be necessary to have intelligent educated people to restore the country after the war was won. And they never quite realized that the war was in a fair way to be lost for at least two years after Pearl Harbor.

I will explain to you. We were having ships sunk in full sight of Atlantic City, on their way into New York. And they were not being torpedoed. The Germans wouldn't waste a torpedo on them. The submarines surfaced and shot them down by gunfire. And the sailors' bodies were washed ashore at Atlantic City. And on the Pacific Coast, when I was out there in '43, everybody had smudge pots in their back yards because they were so afraid of Japanese air raids. A lot of good the smudge pots would have done, but they thought it would, so it gave them some hope.

But the rest of the country I think was ahead of the colleges in admitting the absolute emergency of our situation after Pearl Harbor.

So, there was a slight coolness between Bryn Mawr and myself for some twenty years or so after the war.

Q: Who was head of Bryn Mawr at that time?

Streeter: Miss Katharine McBride. Bryn Mawr of course was a Quaker College. That was —

Q: — that was an element in the picture, too.

Streeter: — the attitude, as far as the trustees were concerned. And you know, I had a funny feeling. I'm not sure the college ever understood I had, but — I felt that they had given no support to the armed forces whatever. Well, I know they didn't. And I know many of the colleges didn't. I went to Bryn Mawr for a recruiting meeting. I think there were perhaps forty people there. I went to the University of California at Los Angeles, there weren't more than that there, although California was a great place for the Marines. I think it was more than a lack of interest. I think - it was frowned upon by the college authorities. Women were certainly not encouraged, undergraduates were not encouraged to go into the armed forces.

Well, as it happened, it didn't hurt the armed forces any. We got all the poeple we wanted. I think perhaps the undergraduates missed something. But we both lived through it.

Then, a sort of entertaining thing happened, because by this time at Bryn Mawr another twenty-five years had gone by. Bryn Mawr was about to have its 75th anniversary, 1960. At the time of the 50th anniversary, I had been on a small and select committee to concentrate on the plans for raising money on that occasion. And I had come up, with a good idea for a way to pay for the new dormitory, which was one of the things that we were trying to raise a great deal of money for.

Q: What kind of endowment did they have up to that point?

Streeter: I don't know. They had an endowment. They were always having drives to raise money for Bryn Mawr, mostly for faculty salaries. But this was to have a dormitory and a new building for the science departments, and it was a time when money was fairly hard to raise, and there were considerable difficulties in the way.

Well, I borrowed this idea from Dartmouth, but I don't think it had ever been tried at Bryn Mawr before. At Dartmouth, they built their dormitories on mortgages, because a dormitory was a money earning building, whereas a science laboratory was not a money earning building nor was a library or buildings of that sort. You couldn't raise your money on a mortgage. But you could get a mortgage on a dormitory because it was always going to be filled and you were always going to make a profit on it.

Very simple idea. Not mine. I borrowed it from somebody else. It's always seemed to me quite stupid to insist on bulling your way through something when somebody has been on that road before and has found a nice way to do it. I borrowed ideas all the way through my life from other people, and furthermore they're very glad to help you, and the only thing is, you must thank them and you must admit that you got the idea from somebody else.

Q: Yes, publicly admit it.

Streeter: Publicly admit it. And I publicly admit, I got **this** idea from Dartmouth College.

Well, it helped very much on the drive because you **didn't** have to raise all the capital sum at once. So I was **temporarily** in good odor at the college. And I suppose when it came to the 75th anniversary, my name must have come up in some way. Anyhow, Miss McBride asked me if I would be chairman of the Alumnae Day Committee, and I did - this was funny, because out of some maybe seven or eight thousand alumnae I was not one! I suggested this to Miss McBride as being inappropriate. But she was a very persuasive person when she put her mind on it. So she talked me into it.

Well, that resulted in our becoming good friends. Up to that point, as I say, there had been a coolness, which I noticed whether the college did or not. And I later learned to like and admire Miss McBride very much. She was a perfectly extraordinary person, and did a great deal for Bryn Mawr, and although I never got to know her very well because we were both occupied with different things, not seeing each other very often, I had a great affection for her and a great admiration for her.

So I sort of came back into the fold a little bit at that time.

Q: And you did head up this committee.

Streeter: Oh, yes. I did.

Q: Along the way you also became a friend of Helen Taft Manning.

Streeter: Oh, yes. I knew Helen Taft long before that. Because she had left college to be in the White House for two or three years. Then she came back to graduate. So she didn't graduate until 1915, and she was a senior at the time that I was a freshman.

The chief thing we had in common was that we were both "mutes." A mute was a person who was requested not to sing within earshot of the campus, because she could put everybody off key without half trying. In those days, we sang a great deal in college, and at senior steps in the spring, the seniors would call on various people to sing. Helen Taft and I were the two worst mutes. And they would every once in a while call on us to sing. My particular song had to do with our freshman show. Our freshman show was laid in Egypt, which is interesting considering all the rage there is now about King Tut. I wrote a great many of the jingles. I never was a poet, but I did write a great many of the jingles, and my roommate saw whether they fitted the tune or not, and I wanted to have some part in the show, which I couldn't see how I was going to do. So, I invented a chorus of mummies, and I put the song to the tune of "The Lone Fish Ball" which is a good old Harvard song and only has three notes in it; but I could never manage to hit even those three!

Q: Well, having successfully served as head of this alumnae committee for the 75th anniversary, what did you do next?

Streeter: Well, I was having increased responsibilities at home so I didn't do much for the college, although I saw Kathy McBride occasionally and her death in 1972 came as a shock to me, as it did to many of us. She was greatly admired and greatly beloved by Bryn Mawr people, as was shown by the memorial service that was held after her death. There were accounts of her administration in the Alumni Bulletin of the summer of 1970 and accounts of the memorial service in the winter Alumni Bulletin of 1977. She had been I think twenty-seven years president, and had been a wonderful president.

Now we have reached 1978 and last spring our class of 1918 held its 60th reunion, and a goodly number were able to return. We also had the pleasure of meeting our new president, Mary Patterson McPherson, who is an able and delightful person. It looks as if the future for private colleges will be difficult, but we all felt that Bryn Mawr was in good hands.

Q: What kind of endowment do they have now?

Streeter: I don't have the answer for the endowment at the present time, but just before Miss McBride died there was a drive for funds and we gathered in 23 million dollars.

Q: Mrs. Streeter, at this juncture, it might be well for you to talk about your brothers and their involvement in World War I. We had reached the year 1917 in your own personal career, your leaving Bryn Mawr.

Streeter: '16, it was.

Q: You left Bryn Mawr in '16, yes. We got involved in 1917 and the boys did also.

Streeter: That's right. By this time, my older brother was still at Harvard and my younger brother was a freshman.

Q: At Harvard also?

Streeter: Yes. The clouds of war were getting darker and darker in Europe. There began to be a good deal of feeling in this country that if we did not help our friends they might well go under. Some of the boys I knew, a little older than the boys still in college, had gone over either in the American Ambulance Corps or some in the Lafayette Escadrille. They were already in the fighting. But this, of course, was only a few men.

On the other hand, preparations were being made in this country. We were getting more and more involved. There was a feeling that the time was coming when we'd have to do something rather drastic.

Harvard had at that time the Harvard Regiment, which was made up of the boys in the undergraduate and graduate schools, and they drilled at Soldiers Field, an appropriate place, and four French officers who had been wounded in the war, came over as instructors. This was quite an event. They came over to Boston on the train, got off at the Back Bay Station, and the Harvard Regiment marched in and met them and marched back to Cambridge with them.

I got ahold of my grandmother, who of course remembered the Civil War very well because she was twenty-five years younger than my grandfather and at this time I think was in her late seventies, and we stood on the edge of the street, on Beacon Street as the parade went by, and of course I was jumping up and down with excitement, recognized a good many of the boys, and I turned to her and I said, "Don't they look wonderful, Grandma? Don't they look wonderful?"

And to my surprise, the tears were rolling down her face. She knew what war was and I didn't.

Q: She had lived through an actual war.

Streeter: She had lived through it. And of course time went on and things got worse. My older brother I guess by that time was in the Harvard Business School, and he had always worn glasses, had poor eyesight, and by the time, the year 1917 rolled around, he tried to enlist, and nobody would have him on account of his poor eyesight. So he was going to try and get into the Quartermaster Corps in the Harvard Regiment.

Meanwhile my younger brother, who had always wanted to fly, and that's the one thing he wanted to do - and in the summer between, I guess it was in the Easter vacation of his sixth form year, he had gone down to Newport News to learn to fly, with my mother's permission, of course.

Q: This was under the aegis of the Army?

Streeter: No, this was a private flying school at that time. And Mother had an idea that the water was a little softer to land on than the ground, which of course was a mistake but I don't think she ever quite realized it. So he started to fly in float planes. And he got quite a little flying in during that vacation. That was what he wanted to do, more than anything else, if war came.

Well, war did come, and immediately, the boys who had been preparing for it tried to put into effect such preparation as they had had. My older brother found that he couldn't even get into the Quartermasters because of his bad eyesight, but at that time some railway engineers were being organized in New England with the Boston and Maine Railroad there, because World War I of course had the miserable idea of a line, a front line, and thank heaven in World War II they did not have front lines. They had learned that the casualties in a static war were just simply awful. But at that time they did have them in World War I, and the regular trains would come up within a reasonable distance of the front - the roads of course were always bad from there to the front, so they used to lay these toy railroads, and they were just like the toys you get for Christmas. They came in strips with the ties attached to the rails, and they were only about, I don't know, two feet wide instead of three or four like the big railways, and they carried the food and ammunition and various needs up as near the front as could be reached without carrying them on your back.

So they were behind the British lines, along the Somme. They did not know at this time of course where they would be sent. They were sent for a little bit of training before they were shipped overseas. Now of course, they never were soldiers. They were railway people and the men were railway men. And Charlie was a private.

Q: Oh, he got accepted into that contingent.

Streeter: He got accepted into that because it didn't make any difference if he wore glasses or not. They were shipped in June of '17, and they were the first Americans to march through London. They were shipped to England because of the advantage in shipping, but then they were marched through London to encourage the British, who by that time were in a bad way. And they did encourage the British, because they were all well grown and well fed and full of energy, and so they marched them through London. But of course, they didn't know anything about marching. First thing they did, they got them in one of the parks which had a fence all around it, and the officer tried to get them out, but he brought them up against the fence every time. Finally he turned around and said, "Gang around and follow me," so he got them out on the street.

But they carried Springfield rifles, which are very heavy, and the company commander never knew enough to change them. So I think they all had sore shoulders by the time that parade was over. However, they did perform their duty as far as encouraging the English was concerned.

And then they were sent to France, and as I say, they operated behind the lines along the Somme. Albert and Amiens - I forget the names of all the places now, but it was along that line that they stayed in the same place for a long time, until, March 1918, when the Germans made their last great attempt to break through the lines. And by gum they did break through the lines.

There was a story shortly after that about how the Portuguese saved Amiens. The British knew that this attack was coming, and they had some Portuguese troops. Portugal was one of our allies. They didn't know what to do with the

the Portuguese troops, and they felt that if they put the British in the front line and the Portuguese as reserves, they might not be there when the reserve was needed. So they put the Portuguese in the front line and the British in the reserve. Then when the attack came and the Portuguese wanted to move, they couldn't move backwards, and so they had to move sideways, and this was a maneuver, military maneuver which was entirely new to the Germans, and they thought it was a trap. So they spent twenty-four hours standing still to try to find out what the Portuguese were doing, and that gave the British time to move up some reinforcements, and therefore they always said that the Portuguese saved Amiens.

Well, meanwhile of course the Germans did break through, and Charlie's regiment we knew was in the thick of it. They were retreating and did have to go back quite a ways. Fortunately they were not involved and he did come safely through that and eventually came safely home. So that was his involvement.

My younger brother Bill, following his inclination to fly, enlisted in the Army. He had this operation on his ears, what's it called? Mastoid operation.

Q: You don't hear about that any more.

Streeter: I know. But it was supposed to upset your sense

of balance. And you had to get a waiver if you wanted to fly, if you'd had a mastoid operation. But he got his waiver and he went to ground school here, and then he was shipped, also, first to France, but then down to Italy to a little place called Foggia on the Adriatic side, where there are many open fields, which is better if you're a student pilot -

Q: - yes, I think so.

Streeter: And they flew of course these planes which, by our standards, were nothing but tied together with chewing gum and string. Bill was among the first to graduate and get his pilot's license, and those pilots, instead of wearing the American silver wings, they wore the Italian gold falcons.

Bill was in charge of the first detachment to go to Foggia and we have a picture of him leading the Americans into the gates of the camp in Foggia.

After he got his wings he became an instructor, and one day when he was up in the air with another boy, they were caught in a cloud, and coming out of the cloud they ran smack into a student who was flying along the edge of the cloud. And all three of them were killed.

They were the first Americans to die in Italy, and quite a little publicity was given to it.

For Bill, of course, this was five days after his 21st birthday. He was not married. He made out his war risk insurance to Mother and me, and we took it and set up an award in the Air Force, United States Air Force, which has been given for well over fifty years now called the Cheney Award. This was set up after World War I, about the middle 1920's, and it goes for unusual valor and self sacrifice in humanitarian work in the Air Force. It's not the sort of a medal that is pinned on your chest for shooting down the enemy. It is largely in peacetime, although sometimes it's given in wartime too. It was not given during World War II. There was too much going on. But it was given in the Korean and Vietnam Wars, and has been given to extraordinary people who have done extraordinary things. Three volumes have been published detailing some of the acts for which it was given. There should be a fourth volume but I have not had the time or energy to publish that. But the Air Force of course keeps the records, and it's entirely within their control. The trust fund yields about a thousand dollars a year, and the Air Force has no interference with whom this award is given.

They have been very appreciative, and for many years Mother and I went down and then later I went down by myself to the presentation, so that I met and knew many of these men and their families. And of late years I have not been able to go down. But it's been a very satisfying thing. It was something that could be done to make up for Bill's loss, something like this, and it's been a great, much more than a pleasure, a deep satisfaction to see the sort of thing that these men do. Many different kinds of things. But many of them have one thing in common. A man will be in a crackup. He will be thrown free or get out of it unscathed himself. He will look back, see all the flames and the ammunition being shot off all over the lot, and he'll see that the other man has evidently been knocked unconscious or something. He'll go back and get him. Now, that takes a very fine spirit, because when you're safe yourself, to go back into that sort of inferno, - there have been several times that it's been given posthumously. It was given to the pilot that flew over Cuba and saw the Russian –

Q: - with the U-2.

Streeter: With the U-2. It's been given for men who landed in the jungle and rescued people in Vietnam and Korea, and many different kinds of things, and it is a wonderful history of the majesty, if you want to call it that, of which human nature is capable - which, in view of all the peculiar things human nature is also capable of, is most encouraging.

And I've had the very deep pleasure of meeting many of these men and their families. I hear from a good many of them still at Christmas time, and also, all the chiefs of staff of the Air Force. In fact, the other day when I let General Allen, the present chief of staff, know that I could not come down this summer for the presentation, he said that he would come and call on me instead. I expected him a couple of weeks ago and it turned out to be a rainy day and he couldn't come into Morristown, but it's a very satisfying, I think is the only word to use for it, experience for the Air Force and for ourselves. General Allen tried again later; and made it this time and we had a most pleasant visit.

Q: What a living memorial to have to your brother!

Streeter: Yes. The wife of an Air Force officer said to me once, she said, "How fortunate you are. You have a continual link with courage."

Q: Did you get involved in any way with World War I?

Streeter: I had a baby.

Q: Oh, I see. All right. We'd better get to that next phase of your life then.

Streeter: No, I didn't do anything myself because this all happened at the same time. Well, I think that's about all there is about World War I. Now we can go back to my private life, if you like.

Q: Yes, indeed.

Streeter: Well, you can see that these years, the years of '17, '18, '19, had a great deal of strain, a great deal of sadness, because of the war. At the same time they had a great deal of excitement and a great deal of delight, because I fell in love, got engaged, got married and began having children.

The way that happened, I had come home from college, had not been interested in being married before, but I was now receptive. I was not necessarily out looking, but I was now receptive. And - what are you laughing about?

Well, anyhow, I think my mother and another lady up in New Hampshire, I've always suspected of putting their heads together. They were good friends and she had a young and attractive and interesting son who was a lawyer in Boston, and his name was Thomas W. Streeter. So Mother somehow got a luncheon together where we met, and this had the results which I think the mothers had hoped would happen. We each kind of took to the other one, and Tom at that time was a lawyer with his own office in Boston.

Q: And he was a Harvard graduate too?

Streeter: Harvard Law School. He was a Dartmouth man but a Harvard Law School graduate. His father was generally known as General Streeter. I discovered that he was not an Army general. He'd been Attorney General of New Hampshire on the Governor's staff, and in those days you know they often appeared in uniform. He was one of the leading lawyers in New Hampshire. He was the lawyer for the Boston and Maine Railroad which ran New Hampshire for some time. He was also a personal lawyer of Mary Baker Eddy, whom (although he was no Christian Scientist) he admired very much. He lived in Concord, New Hampshire. And his wife's father was Alonzo Philetus Carpenter who was Chief Justice of New Hampshire, and Tom's father had gone as a young man to work in the Chief Justice's office. They didn't go to law school in those days, they read law with some lawyer, so -

Q: - which was an awfully good way of getting an education.

Streeter: It certainly is. So this went on for some time and Tom got his law degree and went to work for Choate, Hall, and Stewart, when he got out of Harvard Law School; and Mr. Charles P. Choate, who was the head of the firm, was a man that he admired very much. Later he set up his own office, and it was at that stage of the game that we met.

Shortly after we met, just a few weeks after we met,

he had already been appointed to a mission to South America. I think it was sort of a trade mission. And he was about to start off on that trip. So we didn't see each other for, oh, I guess two or three months, but I would get letters back from South America in which, I'm sorry to say, he kept telling me all about the beautiful senoritas that he was meeting down there.

Q: You said that he got involved with a trade mission to Latin America and was writing back about the senoritas that he fell in with en route.

Streeter: Yes. This began to worry me. But not too much.

Q: It gave you some assessment of your own feelings for him.

Streeter: Yes, it did indeed. Well, then he came back, and we renewed our acquaintance, and this grew into something better, and we became engaged along about April. Then of course that was at the time that the country was also getting into war, and we didn't want to postpone our wedding particularly and so we were married about the middle of June. And I've always regretted that neither of my two brothers could be there. Bill was already in the Army, and Charlie, who was still in the Harvard Regiment, had a test or parade or something that morning, and the car broke down and he couldn't get up in time for the wedding. But -

Q: You were married in Boston?

Streeter: We were married in Peterborough.

Q: In the church your mother had built?

Streeter: The church was not yet finished. So we were married in the big library of the house up on the hill, our home there.

Tom, at that time, was giving up the practice of law as such because he was very much interested in a new job which had been offered him by the American International Corporation. This was a corporation set up by Stone and Webster, the Boston firm, well known for large engineering works, and he became treasurer of it with the offices in New York, which meant of course that we moved to New York. And the first thing, or the biggest thing that the American International was doing at that time was the building of Hog Island. Hog Island was a miserable mud flat in the mouth of the Delaware River, and it had to be built from the mud up, but it was built sort of by an assembly line technique, where they could turn out large numbers of freight ships, small freight ships, and considering the large numbers of freighters that were being sunk by the submarines, this was obviously something that there was great need for in a hurry.

Q: An emergency.

Streeter: An emergency, yes. So he stayed in that job for quite a while, and we had an apartment in New York for a year, and then he wanted to get even more actively interested, and he heard of an opening in the Department of Purchase, Storage and Traffic, which is to say the service of supply in Washington, under General Goethals, and he went down there as head of a division.

So then we moved down to Washington the next winter, and we had a house in Washington which of course at that time was enormously crowded. There were no accommodations for most of the people that came into Washington. They had then what they called "hot bunks" - one man would sleep in the bunk in the daytime, go to work at night, and the other man who had been working all night would come and sleep in the bunk in the daytime. And of course these were horrible conditions, when the war ended and the flu broke out, because of course it just meant that anybody who had the flu gave it to everybody around him.

But for the first period of the war, we lived in the Little Green House on K Street.

Q: Oh, you did, famous for Warren Harding?

Streeter: Which later became famous under President Harding. It was quite a big house. It was green stone, of all things. I think the YMCA is there now.

Q: I remember the green house.

Streeter: Well, of course, it was quite a big house and we had several double guest rooms in it, and we couldn't keep them to ourselves. We didn't need them for ourselves. We felt that we should have somebody there, because people would ring our doorbell and ask us if they could possibly have a room, and so we took two friends of ours who were majors in the Ordnance Department in the Army. One of them was a great big husky and he had been on the gold rush to Alaska, and had climbed up that awful trail from Skagway. He was kind of a venturesome soul. But anyhow -

Q: - and he must have appealed to you.

Streeter: Sure. They were both married. They were friends of Tom's and they were married, and of course they were considerably older than I was. Tom was 11 years older than I was. And they were - let's see, one couple had no children. The other, their children were grown. So the two couples moved in with us. But as it was our house, I did the housekeeping. And I'd only been married about a year and a half by that time, had a small baby, knew nothing about housekeeping in a house.

Q: And hadn't been especially trained for that kind of a job, had you?

Streeter: Well, yes. We got training in housekeeping.

Q: Did you?

Streeter: Oh, yes. I was no cook but I knew how to tell the cook how to run the meal. We got some maids down from New York, as a matter of fact, because they were mostly black in Washington, and I didn't know too much about them. But here I was, running a house for two older families, and I've always had a real affection for those two wives, because I'm sure either one of them could have run the house much better than me. But they were paying board and lodging, the only profitable housekeeping I ever kept in my life.

The reason it went so well was that I found out what the two men wanted particularly, and they got plenty of it. One of them liked Spanish omelet and he got Spanish omelet I guess every other day. The other one -- I think he liked popovers or something of that sort and he got those every meal. So we lived along, quite comfortably.

How did the wives manage, or did they get involved in

war work?

Streeter: Oh yes, they got involved in war work, and as I say, they really were very nice. So this was '17, '18.
Let's see - the war ended in '18, didn't it?

Q: Yes.

Streeter: This was '17 and '18. And as I say, we had the flu in '18, and that -

Q: Did that strike your household?

Streeter: Well, not particularly. But we all did war work. The way Washington was organized at that time, they had a center in each of the four quarters of Washington. There was a high school and that was the center. So these two women volunteered to go down and cook at one of the centers, and their two husbands were entitled to a car, and they had got the car with a sergeant to drive them. The sergeant took it one time without any particular permission and rather smashed it up. So they didn't keep him after that. It was the Model T Ford, and nobody else of the six of us except me could drive a Model T Ford. So I inherited the Model T Ford, and I would go down with the other wives to the school, and then I would take the food, take it around and distribute it.

Q: As a footnote, how did you acquire a knowledge of driving a Model T?

Streeter: Well, I think we had a Model T. Not Tom and I, but my family.

Q: Your family did.

Streeter: Before. Yes. I think it was a little different from gear shifts, ordinary gear shifts, but it was all right.

So then I remember of course Armistice Day, that year, and we went down. We had some captured German cannon out by the Capitol. We all went down and made rude remarks to the captured German cannon.

Of course we were vastly relieved and delighted when that war came to an end. Meanwhile, I had had quite a trying time at one period, because I was no sooner married than I became pregnant, and of course, I was about seven months along I guess when Bill was killed, and that was not easy. And then our oldest son was born in March, when I knew that my other brother was in the middle of the German advance. And these times were pretty difficult. But he got out all right and the baby got along all right, and that was the first of several. He's now 61 years old and doing very well.

We stayed I think until the first part of 1919, and

Streeter #2 - 96

then we came back to New York. Frank was born in New York. Then, our -

Q: - did your husband go back to the law?

Streeter: No, he never went back to law. He stayed in business, banking or other business. I think the first business he went into about this time was oil. The Stone and Webster people had interests in an oil company, of which at one time he became president. It was a Texas oil company. Our fortunes ebbed and flowed to some extent after this. As Tom used to explain to me, if you've inherited money, that's all right, you can conserve money, but if you haven't inherited money, you have to try to make money, and sometimes it works and sometimes it doesn't.

Q: You inherited money. Had he inherited money also?

Streeter: I'd inherited a little. I hadn't inherited very much by that time. He had oil interests down in Mexico, in Tampico of all places, and I could tell you stories about that for a long time, but I won't at this particular stage.

Q: You might tell me the fact that there he hooked up with the father of the present Buckley clan.

Streeter: Oh yes. One of our ushers, one of our friends was Will Buckley, who was the father of Bill Buckley the commentator at the present time. He was the partner that was down in Tampico and Tom was more or less the financial end up in New York. Tampico was, I gather, a pretty messy place in those days, because it was pretty swampy.

Q: It's not better now. Not much.

Streeter: Did I tell you the story about the twelve honest judges and the twelve corrupt judges?

Q: You mentioned that, yes.

Streeter: Do you want to hear that?

Q: Yes.

Streeter: Well, among other properties there, as well as oil wells, the two had bought an island in the middle of the river, which was to be filled in and used for warehouses and supply stations like that. They had a little trouble with the local ward leaders about that, and as is customary in Mexico, they had to bribe them a little, and they got their various permits. They kept in reasonably close and friendly touch with this ward heeler. In Tampico.

Time went on and conditions changed, and there was some question about their title to the island, which was appealed to the courts, up to the Supreme Court of Mexico, which at that time was popularly supposed to consist of twelve honest judges and twelve corrupt judges.

The President of Mexico at that time got in touch with them and said, "Is there any way I can be of assistance to you?"

They did a double take and realized that this was Portes Gil, who was the little ward heeler, who was now the President of Mexico!

So this was fine, and they said, "Yes, we've got a good case. The twelve honest judges will be for us, if you'll just take care of the twelve corrupt judges."

So I think they cleared their title to the island in Tampico.

This was the sort of thing more or less that went on in Mexico in those days.

Q: You said that Will Buckley was an usher at your wedding?

Streeter: Yes.

Q: Had he been a friend of - ?

Streeter: He and Tom had been in oil before. Will was an

Irish Texan, and that was a wonderful combination. He was a wonderful old pirate and I always liked him very much. I'm not too sure just how his behavior was in all of these matters, but he was quite a cheerful sinner anyhow. I was specially fond, I am still specially fond of his wife, Aloise, because he got engaged to her in Tampico soon after we were married, and wrote up to me and said, "I've just met the most wonderful girl and we're going to be married. I want to give her an engagement ring and I can't find anything in Tampico. She wants a solitaire diamond. Will you get it and send me down the ring?"

Well, of course I didn't have the slightest idea what sort of girl he might be engaged to.

Q: Was she a Texan also?

Streeter: Oh no, she was a New Orleans girl, and so, I consulted with Tom as to what amount to spend approximately. He gave me a figure, and I went and got a solitaire diamond in a very simple setting, because it seemed to me that if she ever wanted a more elaborate setting, that wouldn't cost too much, and the value was in the diamond. But I've always been very pleased that she never changed the setting. We saw them off and on, in the years later, when they lived in Sharon, Connecticut.

So we had those oil experiences in Mexico. Then

Tom got involved in a tin mine in Alaska. Tin at that time was a metal that was very much needed for cans. We didn't have frozen stuff, of course, and most of the tin was in Malaya, so this alleged mountain of tin was in Alaska, and we put considerable money into the tin mine, and I suspect that it had been salted; at least it turned out eventually that there was insufficient tin to make it worthwhile. So we had to cross off our losses, cross off the tin mine.

And I couldn't have been more entertained, to hear later on in World War II, that some other damn fool had bought the tin mine.

Q: The same mine?

Streeter: The same mine, and sold it to the United States government, which also found there was insufficient tin in it. If they'd bothered to ask us, we could have told them.

Well, that annoyed Tom very much. Of course, the Alaskans in those days, and I'm not sure that it doesn't persist to some extent still, felt that anybody from the lower forty-eight states was fair game. So, Tom decided he was going to get some of his money back out of Alaska if it was in any way possible. So he bought various gold leases of one sort of another, on the beach at Nome and back of Nome, and on the Ungalik River. These were placer mines, and the Ungalik was the only one that really turned up much.

And it did produce a modest profit. It was interesting and sort of fun, because we had to get a dredge up there by sections. It of course had to come up in a freighter, and it had to be floated ashore in barges, no real harbor, of course. Then it had to come over the tundra in a thing called a "Go Devil" which I suppose was some sort of tracked vehicle, and then it had to be put together again in the river.

You only have 100 days in Alaska when you can work, so they always worked 24 hours a day seven days a week, and they get enormous pay but they work for it.

Of course, the first thing you have to do in that part of Alaska and that kind of a mine is, you have to thaw the ground, because a foot or two down, it's solid ice. So you thaw the ground by sinking pipes, and then running the river water through the pipes, pumping it through. That thaws it. Then you get the layer of soil that is over the gold bearing sands, you scoop it out with the dredge. Then you run the sand through the dredge along pans that have mercury in them, and it picks up the gold dust. This was dust and not nuggets. Not nuggets.

Well, it worked pretty well. The first year our oldest son, Frank, went up and worked there. Then a couple of years later our second son, Henry, went up and worked there. I'm not sure whether Tommy ever got to or not. I'm not sure he did. But anyhow, eventually World War II came along, and we had always — you send your food and your supplies up by freight, by boat, one summer, and then they are there by the next summer, and you fly your men up the next summer. So, the government confiscated all our supplies and machinery when World War II broke out, and was glad to have them in that part of Alaska, without having to transport them up.

Q: Did your husband ever go up there?

Streeter: He never did. No. I tried to go once but the weather was so bad they wouldn't fly me down. But the boys, I think all of them, yes, I'm sure Tommy went up too. I think all of them worked up there, each one summer in the 1940s.

Then, we went back after World War II, and we got a little more out one year, but by that year it was pretty well exhausted. But it was a great experience for the kids, and it was sort of fun for everybody, and it paid off enough to be worth it.

Q: Did it recoup the losses from the tin?

Streeter: I'm not sure about that. But anyhow it was quite an experience.

Well, to go back to where we were immediately after

World War 1 - this was all I suppose in the early twenties and so on. We had peaks and shoals, as I said. We had one son born in 1918, one born in 1920 and one born in 1922. By that time, we thought it was time to move out of the city.

We had been having a prosperous era, prior to 1922, for a year or two, and we had sublet, I mean we had rented from one of the Lehmans a very handsome house at 16 East 81st Street. It's now the town house of Governor Harriman. We were a little out of our class!

Our prosperity didn't last that long. So that was another reason for moving out of New York to a place that we hoped would be a little less expensive to live in. And who do you think sublet the house on 81st Street from us? The N. B. Whites!

So we had an interesting time at least. Then we came out to Morristown, and --

Q: - how did you select Morristown?

Streeter: Well, we went around. We first decided that there was no point in bringing up three boys in the city. And so we drove around. We went out to Westchester. We went out to Connecticut. We went out to Long Island. We went down on the Jersey Shore. And we came to Morristown. And we just liked the feel of Morristown better than any of the others. It is not a suburb of anything. It is not a resort. It has its own history and its own self respect. In those days it wasn't crowded, the way it is now, and we just liked the feel of it. We had one or two friends here but not very many. We rented a great big house, because we could see we were going to have a great big family. Eventually after my husband's death I tore it down and came to live in a little cottage on the same place.

Q: Not so small at that. How many - ?

Streeter: - well, I find the quarters upstairs very convenient.

Q: How many did you say you could sleep at one time?

Streeter: Nine. I've got nine beds upstairs, but that's for grandchildren. I've lived here now fifty-seven years. In Morristown. And enjoyed it very much, always very glad that we moved out here. For a good many years we all were here and enjoyed it. And then of course the next thing that happened was, the roof fell in, in '29. I don't mean the real roof.

Q: You mean, the financial roof.

Streeter: I mean the financial roof.

Q: But before that time you began to get involved, in spite of the fact that you had very small children, you began to get involved in local activities.

Streeter: Oh yes. I did.

Q: Would you focus on them for a moment? That began with - ?

Streeter: Well, that began in, I think, a little less than a year after we moved out. The doorbell rang one day, and when I answered the door, it was Mrs. Paul Moore, whom I did not know very well then, although she's become one of my best friends out here since then. She had come to ask me if I would be president of the Morristown Visiting Nurse Association.

Q: And what were your credentials for Mrs. Moore to come and ask that?

Streeter: I have never been able to find out why she particularly thought of me in that connection. But she did, and as I have mentioned before, I have a sporting spirit about this sort of thing when I'm asked. It never seems to have occurred to me that I might not be able to do the job. So I've always tried. That's been my motto - you can always try. Occasionally it's led to my falling flat on my face, but, a certain number of times it's succeeded reasonably well. So anyhow, I did accept this, and I accepted in some terms which I should not have used. I said that I was interested in nursing and that I was not interested and never would be interested in social service, because social work involved your telling people how to run their lives and they always resented it. The one thing they didn't resent was, if they were sick, being looked after and made comfortable. So I would be willing to go into nursing but not into social work.

I should never say "never", because I spent about the next fifteen or twenty years in social work.

However, I did begin by nursing. And I guess I was president of the Visiting Nurses Association about four years, and then I found I was pregnant again, and our small daughter arrived, whom we'd been waiting for for some time, having had three boys, and who has been a delight to us ever since.

I'm by no means able to keep up with her, in all the things she does, but I watch in admiration. And our three boys of course have been something special to us too.

So there we were, all settled in Morristown, and I'd begun to have a little spare time and to think of doing things outside.

Well, after I resumed my outside labors, after Lil was born, I was put on the State Board of Children's Guardians. This was not one of my more successful efforts.

Q: What is this, Children's Guardians?

Streeter: Children's Guardians - well, I think we had about 40,000 children, about 20,000 with their mothers and 20,000 in foster homes or institutions. They were the state program.

Q: Oh, I see, foster home program.

Streeter: It was at that time rather disorganized. It was being run out of Jersey City, which is in the northeast corner of the state of New Jersey, and how you're going to cover the whole state from there - most state organizations are in Trenton, which is at the narrow center of the state where you can go in both directions.

Well, we had a peculiar kind of government in New Jersey in those years. These were the days of the Hague Machine. Frank Hague of course was Mayor of Jersey City, and he was rather an unattractive cuss himself. I don't think he ever could have been elected to anything much anywhere except Jersey City. But he had a wonderful partner, A. Harry Moore. Everybody liked A. Harry Moore, and the Republicans liked him as well as the Democrats. But in those days a governor could not succeed himself. He could be governor any number of times so long as he didn't succeed himself. So we were appointed by a Republican governor. Then we had Harry Moore, and with his Jersey City connections, there were going to be no more reforms anywhere while he was governor.

So I felt that I was in a dead end there and only served one term.

Then we had a Republican governor. Then we had A. Harry Moore again. Then we had another Republican governor, and then we had Harry Moore a third time.

Q: Were the Republican governors different each time, or did they just swap offices?

Streeter: Oh, I think they were different. But we had Harry Moore three times. And he was quite a good governor, escept that he did see eye to eye with Mayor Hague on most things.

But, the thing I learned, I certainly make mistakes from time to time but I try to learn something from them, and I learned my way abound Trenton a little bit. More of what not to do and what to do than I had known when I first went down there. Also I got acquainted with various people down there.

Well, next thing that happened was the Depression, the great Depression, and anybody that wasn't, you know, reasonably grown up in '29 and the early thirties doesn't know what we went through then. Much worse than anything that there's ever been since. Because we've had welfare since, generous welfare, I may say.

Q: A cushion.

Streeter: We didn't have anything like that. Money was practically out of circulation. People would barter, people who lived in the country would barter their pigs and their vegetables and all for kerosene for their stoves for the winter. People who were on welfare got enough for food and clothes and lodging depending on the size of their family. They were given work of a certain number of days a week depending on the size of their family. A single man would get maybe two days' work a week. A man with a large family would get five or six days' work a week. And you've not heard of anything like that ever since. They all get the going rate for the whole week.

I think that was perhaps too drastic. But I wish that the people who are running welfare now would at least go back to some of the people who had some experience then and try to work out something part way between what we've got now and what we had then.

In those days, the State Relief Council couldn't succeed in pleasing everybody, couldn't succeed in pleasing anybody, with the net result that they rotated rather rapidly, and no one would last more than about one year.

Well, I was the only woman on the State Relief Council along about 1932 or '33, and it was of course a very interesting, rather strenuous affair. We got mobbed one day. We were inside the building so it didn't hurt us particularly, but we were mobbed. One thing I'm really afraid of is a mob. I've always been, as I told you, a little disappointed that not one mugger has ever annoyed me, because I think I could take care of one mugger, but --

Q: - don't be too sure.

Streeter: One. Not more than one. But I am afraid of a mob. They are completely carried away.

Q: Unpredictable.

Streeter: Well, all you can predict is bloody murder.

These people from a labor camp up the river were marching through on a labor march to Washington, and could they go through Trenton without having sidewalk speeches? No, they couldn't. And so they were outside the building while we were meeting, and soap box orators were getting more and more het up.

I was sitting in the window watching with the head of the state CIO, who was one of our board members, and he pointed out a couple of men that were not in the front row, not making speeches, sort of standing on the doorstep, and he said, "You know who's really running this riot?"

I said, "No." He said, "Those two men."

"The soap box orators are not the people who are running this riot." And he was right. He said that the police were going to have to stop this very soon or it would get completely out of hand. And they did. They had to wade in with their night sticks, before it got completely out of hand.

That was an interesting sidelight.

Q: What were some of the problems you had to deal with on this Commission?

Streeter: Feeding people. That's all we had to deal with.

Q: Feed the people in terms of numbers.

Streeter: Yes. You know, and allowances and all that. And we had the PWA and we had the CCC and we had all those things.

Q: The funds, they were largely federal funds that you were - ?

Streeter: Yes, largely, but administered by the state.

Q: Now, how much time did you have to give to this job?

Streeter: Well, we met in Trenton. I guess we met about once a week, certainly every two weeks, all day, had sandwiches sent in. It was a fairly strenuous job.

Q: And did you have to do traveling around the state, to view the program in operation?

Streeter: Well, I did that, both with the Board of Guardians and with this, to some extent. But this was more of a top echelon.

I'll tell you sort of an interesting occurrence that happened in connection with this. At the time, Edison was running for President.

Q: Charles Edison?

Streeter: Charles Edison. I mean he was running for governor. He wasn't any particular good but he was a Democrat. And so President Roosevelt agreed, he was on his way to New York by train, he agreed to stop off at an all day conference that was being held in Newark by Mr. Edison, presided over by Mr. Edison, and give his blessing to him in fact.

So I was there. There must have been three or four hundred people, I should think, and Roosevelt came in, on the arm of his bodyguard, and sat down in a comfortable chair. Mrs. Roosevelt was there, and Edison was presiding. And it was understood that Roosevelt was not to be asked to speak. Oh, I think he said - I don't know that he said anything when he came in, because the conference was already under way. And he was not to be asked to speak. And of course, I think he would have wrung Edison's neck, because after an hour or so, and it was obvious that the President was getting ready to leave, Edison turned to him and said, "Mr. President, I know that we're not supposed to ask you to speak, but I think these good people would be very much disappointed if you wouldn't even say one word to them."

Well, the President was way at the front of the stage. His bodyguard was way at the back of the stage. He couldn't get up by himself. His chair had arms to it. He turned around and knelt on the seat of his chair and hauled himself to his feet and came to the front of the stage in the face and eyes of 400 people.

Q: Which he never liked to do.

Streeter: Never liked to do. But with complete aplomb, came to the podium and spoke. But I bet he wrung Edison's neck afterwards for it. But I said to myself - I knew him a little bit, and I didn't always like him, but you had to hand it to him for the way he handled his disability. And that I really was impressed by, and I guess a good many other people were too.

Well, we got fired. We had about a year and we got fired. Somebody else got put in, lasted about another year, and gradually things worked out of the Depression. But it was a very very difficult time.

And Tom lost his job. I mean, the job disappeared. He didn't lose it, it disappeared. He was fortunate enough to get another, settling the Bank of the United States, which was bankrupt, and he --

Q: Was that located in New York?

Streeter: Yes. He got as much money out of that for the people who lost their money as could be gotten. And then he settled another bankrupt organization, and this all took him I guess a couple of years. Yes, this must have taken him more than that, because it was now getting on to be '39.

This Depression lasted a long time, you know.

Q: It certainly did.

Streeter: A lot of people went bankrupt. A lot of organizations went bankrupt. The second one was a court-approved reorganization, and every week, every Thursday, the people who had been appointed by the court would meet, and Tom would have to report to them what had happened the previous week. And they were not very good appointees and there was always a hassle every Thursday. And this was wearing him out. You know, he couldn't really get anything done the way he wanted it done, and he'd got, by this time all except the very little bits, he'd recovered what was recoverable.

So he came out one day and he said, "You know, I'd like to give up going to work."

He was 56, 57 at that time I think. He said, "I think that I can manage to support the family by investments. I've learned enough about investments so that I think I can look after the family all right, and I'd like to give it up. I'm tired of commuting in to New York and I'm tired of this hassle."

I said, "Well, okay, Tom. What do you want to do?"

He'd always wanted to be an historian and a book collector, ever since he was in college, and of course naturally he'd had to leave that to one side, when he was in the law and when he was in active business. So, he did just that. He came out here, and he started a whole new career for the next twenty-five years of his life. And enjoyed it thoroughly, which I was delighted to have him do. He worked, over in the big house. He had a great big room and he had a librarian and a secretary, and he had a wonderful time. He wrote a bibliography of Texas in three volumes. He studied the period up to the Mexican War. He didn't get into the Mexican War. He collected a great many books, not only on Texas but also on - he had the Columbus Letter. He had the Pigaffeta, the diary of Magellan's voyage around the world via the Straits, and he had first books from every one of the forty-eight states, and he built up this really famous library. Oh, he was president of the Grolier Club, President of the Bibliographical Society of America, member of the Walpole Club. He was treasurer of the New York Historical for years. I guess he was a "friend" of every college library pretty nearly in the country. And he was having a wonderful time. He eventually pulled together this really quite famous collection. And he had told me, and had told other people who were book collectors, that when he died, he was not going to leave this all to some single college or university library, he wanted it to be sold at auction. He'd had so much fun pulling it together that he thought a lot of other people would have fun.

So eventually it went for auction at Parke-Bernet, in seven different auctions, for a gross of $3,100,000. At that time this was a tremendous sum.

Q: He was still living?

Streeter: Oh no. He was dead. And I was one of his executors, and I always said I didn't know anything about his books, because you've really got to know a lot about them or not much, you know, and I didn't have the brains or the interest to go into it in depth, and I don't think he would have liked me to go into it in depth, that was his -

Q: That was his province.

Streeter: Right. And so, we had three advisors who were book dealers, and they couldn't have been more surprised when they discovered how much I did know about the collection, when it came to appraising it and to planning —

Q: — yes, I can't imagine you operating —

Streeter: — I'd been living with the darned thing for twenty-five years. And all of these men used to come out and see the collection, you know, and spend the night, and I'd look after them and all that, so we all knew each other pretty well, and I had absorbed a certain amount of information.

Q: I don't think you've ever operated in a vacuum.

Streeter: Well, in any case, I think he had a very happy time, and I was delighted, and he certainly never did neglect his family.

Q: And supported them well enough too.

Streeter: Yes. He did indeed. So he lived to be 81, nearly 82, and so this went on for a long time.

Q: Oh really? There's one other item I'd like to go back to — you were talking about the various activities in that period of the twenties and during the Depression. You're listed also as having been involved in the Morris County Welfare Board. Tell me about that, if you will?

Streeter: Yes. That was one of the things that went along parallel to other things, more or less. I've forgotten the exact dates, but I would think, about 1932-41.

Q: '33 to '41 is the date I have, but there's a question mark.

Streeter: No, '32 to '41.

Q: I see.

Streeter: In any case, this was quite interesting, and it was a spin off from the Depression. Up until then, we'd had Poor Masters, you know, in each municipality.

Q: And the county poor house, I suppose.

Streeter: Oh yes, the county poor house. And these municipal welfare people, as they were later called, had no training, in most cases. They were somebody who was on the municipal pay roll and didn't have anything in particular else to do. Most of them were part time. And they were all right when you weren't in the middle of a Depression, but they were not really trained, or had the background to cope with the large scale trouble that we were having in the Depression.

Q: I suppose they weren't cognizant of resources, either.

Streeter: No. And as the Depression began to wane a little, it was still a heavy work load, and the feeling on the part of a good many people in that field was that we should have a county board with trained investigators who would handle this situation.

Now, we had had to some extent trained investigators for what, in those days, we didn't mince words - we called them the permanent poor and the temporary poor. And the permanent poor were people who were disabled, old age, we were beginning to have old age security then - it came in in the middle thirties, you know. Didn't have it before then. And also the Children's Guardians. Things like that. They had some trained social workers, but the temporary poor did not. And there was a provision, in a law that was passed about that time, that by referendum, any county could set up a County Welfare Board, which would take care of both the temporary and the permanent poor, if they so wished.

Well, the only two that did were Sussex, which is a little country county up here, and Morris. It was interesting, how we got it done in Morris, because we put on a real campaign. Women's clubs helped, the Kiwanis and Rotary and those kinds of clubs helped, civic clubs, and then we got both the Democrats and the Republicans to help, strangely enough. Our state senator was named Frank Abell. He was a Republican and a very fine man. He was in favor of it. A great influence in the Democratic Party, although he was not an office holder, was Judge Holland, who -- because he saw the bad effects of not having proper care of these people end up in his court, more or less. So he was in favor of it.

This was all very helpful indeed. One day the president of the Women's Club and I went to see Judge Holland. The Women's Club was going to have a special meeting to discuss this referendum, you see, and I was to speak, we wanted to get the Judge to speak, both in favor of it.

So the Judge sat down, looking like an owl, and finally he said to the president, "Well, Madame, I will be very glad to speak at your meeting, under one condition."

She said, "What's that?"

And he said, "I would like please to speak before Mrs. Streeter, because by the time Mrs. Streeter has dealt with a subject, there is very little left to say about it."

You see, I get a lot of this as time went by. But it was certainly all said good naturedly and I certainly took it good naturedly. The Judge and I were good friends.

So, after it was approved by referendum and started up here, Senator Abell became president the first year and

I was here, Senator Abell became president the first year and I was vice president. He had told me, "I'll start it off, but after that you've got to take it over."

So then I became president and I was president for eight years more. That brought me up to '41.

Q: What sort of clientele did you build up, in numbers?

Streeter: Oh, I couldn't tell you. It's still going strong, of course. I haven't any idea. It wasn't numbers, it was the amount of time it took.

Q: Yes. How did you manage this simultaneously with some of these other things you were doing, and also the family?

Streeter: Well, I've seldom been running less than a five ring circus at once. If I'm only running a three ring circus, I feel sort of lazy.

Q: You did have adequate help in the house and with the children.

Streeter: Yes, I did. I was fortunate about that. At the present time, the lady that served us has been with me about sixty years, raised her family, her own children, her grandchildren, and her great-grandchildren have been born in the apartment over the garage out there.

The man who works for me was a sergeant in the German Army in World War II for five years. He's been with me over thirty years. I've been very fortunate in having people that I could depend on.

Q: Yes, that did free your hands to a certain extent.

Streeter: Oh yes. Absolutely. I mean, if I'd had to be preparing meals, actually day to day, take care of the children when they were littler or supervision of them - but they did not lack supervision, and I think -

Q: - just as you in your youth didn't lack -

Streeter: - did not either. And this is what's happening now. The children come home from school, half past three, half past four - nobody's there, and nobody watches them, until time for dinner when their father, and usually their mother now also, come home. And this is the time where vandalism so often occurs. Got nothing else they can think of to do, which to my way of thinking is absolutely no excuse for knocking down mail boxes and grave stones, and vandalism and all that sort of thing. They never were paddled properly when they were young.

Q: That is a remedy, isn't it? You said you acquired something which you mother always had, and I think you should tell me on tape.

Streeter: Well, I call it the Voice of Authority. Now, this is not something that you come by easily. You have to earn it. But if you do manage to acquire it, it saves a great deal of dissension. Only you mustn't use it too often and you must be careful to keep your sense of humor.

Q: Thank you.

Interview with Mrs. Ruth Cheney Streeter
Mrs. Thomas W. Streeter, Sr.
At her home, Morristown, New Jersey
June 18, 1979
By John T. Mason, Jr.

Q: It's delightful to be with you again this morning. We're going to lap back a bit in time this morning, and it's your intention, I believe, to talk about the family side of your life, during or after your marriage, and on up to the period when you became a lady Marine. So we'll go back to the time of your marriage in 1917.

Mrs. Streeter: That's a long time ago now, Mr. Mason. But it's nice to have you here, and I'm glad that the air conditioning is working, so we can have a pleasant conversation.

I am glad to go back to my family, because I think that is perhaps one of the things that is of interest to people nowadays, the fact that I could have the leisure to do a lot of outside activities, and yet have the main part of my life be my family life.

Q: Yes. It has been an incredible kind of career. But on

the surface, one would think almost an impossible career, to have done all the things you did and still raise a family.

Mrs. Streeter: Well, I had a very good help. And what happens in many ways, if you lead the type of life as I did in those days - you have to be versatile yourself, because the people who help you are good at one thing, one year, and then there's a change and the next person is good at something else, and your job is to fill in the chinks, no matter who your helper is. Somebody who disciplines the children rather severely, then I have to make up to them by coddling them a little bit, and if they coddle them too much, then I have to come across with a little discipline.

Q: In other words, you orchestrate the whole thing.

Streeter: Yes. I keep the balance. And then also of course, in housekeeping, there are a great many chores that are routine, have to be done all the time, but are time consuming.

Q: And have to be supervised.

Streeter: And energy consuming. And so, I was very fortunate, as I confided to you a little while ago - I never cooked my own meals until I was 70 years old. And went to live in a little house by myself where there wasn't any room for anybody else.

But I survived even that, as you see.

Well, going back to the early 1920's, our first son, Frank, was born in 1918. Our second son Henry was born in '20, and our third son Tommy was born in '22. Then there was a five year gap, making ten years in all, and as I look back over old family pictures, and remember all the things we did, there was a whole ten years when I had nothing but masculine influence around me.

Then in 1927, our daughter was born. And there are all sorts of things that happened during those ten years that she had no part in. But she is quite a gal. She's certainly had a lively part in everything since.

Well, I think I brought us up to the point where we had lived in New York, and after the third boy arrived, decided to come to Morristown where we could turn them out to graze in the field by themselves.

Q: Where you could raise them more properly.

Streeter: Well, let them grow up without constant supervision and develop their own intiative about things.

Another reason was that by that time, things were getting a little tight in our family (1921-22). We had lean years and fat years. And we had had a fat year. We were living at 16 East 81st St., which is now Governor Harriman's town house, and we rented this mansion.

Q: How many rooms did that have?

Streeter: Well, it was quite a mansion. It belonged to one of the Lehman family. My husband had a great many interests. He had oil interests. He had interests in Alaska. At that time, we had leases on a tin mine. The tin mine turned out to have been salted. There wasn't any real tin in it. Somebody had planted some when we weren't around to take the assay.

Q: You mean it was a fraud.

Streeter: Well, it was a fraud, sure. Any good Alaskan will tell you that the greatest fun is to skin the people from the Lower 48.

Q: Was there any recourse in law, your husband being a lawyer?

Streeter: Well, I don't think that helped any, because the Alaskans in those days had their own law, too. But it made him mad, so he was going to get his money back out of Alaska if it was the last thing he ever did. So he went into gold leases after that, and that was a lot of fun.

But just to finish up the story of the Lost River Tin Mine, we let it go for taxes, having discovered that there was no tin in it, and didn't follow it particularly. And then, to our astonishment, in World War II, when they needed tin badly, most of the tin was in Malaysia and they couldn't get it and they needed it badly, so the government got stung too about the Lost River Tin Mine. They bought it up and there wasn't any tin in it. If they'd asked us, we could have told them. We didn't know about it.

Q: Had it been lying dormant all those years?

Streeter: Sure. There wasn't any tin in it. Nobody had done anything to it. Well, anyhow, we had better luck with the gold mines. And we took up leases.

Q: It was panning gold?

Streeter: Panning. But most of the rivers had been panned by hand, so that the surface gold had been taken up. But the -

Q: - a great influx of people looking for fortunes up there, wasn't there?

Streeter: Yes, but that was over by the time we went in,

which was later than what I'm talking about now. This was in the thirties. And you had to dredge. And the overburden, as they call it, the gravel, was about six feet deep or so, and frozen, of course, with permafrost, so you had to have a dredge to dig down through that. Then the gold would be between, at the bottom of the gravel, against the rock or whatever the subsurface was. Then you dug it up and you put it over mercury beds, and you got the dust, the gold dust.

Well, later on, of course, we're in the mining, we might as well finish that, our three boys went up, each one one summer, to work on the gold mine, and this was quite an experience (1936-40). Frank went up the summer after his fresman year, and I think each of the other boys did too, and in Alaska, you work 100 days, and you work twelve hour days or twenty-four if necessary.

Q: The sun is shining all that time.

Streeter: Certainly. The sun is shining. You can't work very much longer than that. This was up by Nome. Our mines were up near Nome. Mostly the best one was on the Ungalik River, which is a little southeast of Nome.

Q: How many mines did you have at one time?

Streeter: We didn't have any other mines. We didn't mine

any of the others, but we had leases. And you drill them to see, you make checkerboard drills to see if there's enough color to put in a dredge.

Q: Just as they do for oil, they drill.

Streeter: Yes. Same sort of thing. So there appeared to be some at the Ungalik. And what you do, of course, first we had to get the dredge up in pieces, the dredge being a rather heavy piece of machinery, and of course, the bay wasn't anywhere near where the mine was, so that stuff had to be lightered ashore. Then we had what was called a "go devil," with a track, that lugged it, with boats, stone boats sort of, across the tundra, to where the river was. Then it had to be bolted together again.

So the first summer, when Frank was up there, we didn't actually get very much gold mined.

Q: Took almost the 100 days to get the equipment there.

Streeter: Pretty near. And then of course, you had to have your food and all your supplies, too. Then later, what you did was to fly up the men and the food. Well, you shipped up the food by boat the last part of one summer, and left it there, and the oil and all that.

Q: That stayed there all winter long?

Streeter: Yes. People didn't steal it. And then you flew your men up.

Q: You had to build houses for them?

Streeter: Shacks of sorts. Not palaces by any means.

And then, you flew your men up early in June. Later one time, I flew up to Nome, and I wanted to go down to the mine, but it was so rough that nobody would take me, and the first ship was just coming into Nome, on the longest day of the year. Nome of course has no harbor. It's just all shore. They were just beginning to bring supplies ashore. They had the longest day, 23rd of June.

So you got your men up, and you had your supplies already there, so you could begin, and that saved a lot of time, because if you had to wait till the men came up by boat, you see, you couldn't start too soon.

Then come World War II, the government confiscated all our supplies that we'd flown up there, the end of the summer, and we were glad that they were there and available for them.

Q: Did you get compensation for the supplies?

Streeter: I suppose so. I don't really remember. But we got enough out of the mine to more than cover expenses, and make a little bit, but we didn't make any great fortune out of it.

Q: Did you recoup the loss from the tin mine?

Streeter: Well, I assume we did. I never did go into that too closely, but --

Q: Was that a touchy point with your husband?

Streeter: That was quite a touchy point. But anyhow, some of his oil things and all came through, so by the middle of the 1920's we were doing quite well.

Q: He didn't make many mistakes in that area, did he?

Streeter: Well, he made one or two good ones, but then he recouped them afterwards. As he used to explain to me, there's a lot of difference between conserving money and making money. If you're going to make money, you've got to take a few risks. I thought that was perfectly all right.

Q: Well, the man who gave us the Parable of the Talents knew that.

Streeter: Yes, and I've never understood the Parable of the Talents.

Q: Your husband was saying another version of that.

Streeter: Yes. Yes, he understood it all right. But you see, none of the people to whom the owner had given the talents lost them. Now, what would he have done if some of them had lost them?

Q: Well, consider the fact that the man buried one of them. That was almost the equivalent of losing it.

Streeter: Oh no, it's not. Oh no, it's not, I can tell you that —

Q: Well, he didn't get a real accolade for doing so.

Streeter: No, he got scalped because he didn't add to it. But I've always wondered what the owner would have said if he'd gone into debt for it or something. Anyhow, that's one of the parables that I've never entirely understood.

Well, in any case, we got our fun out of Alaska, and the boys got a lot of good experience.

Q: They must have had some great tales to tell when they went back to Harvard.

Streeter: Oh yes. Gee, I don't know if I have them. I

wish I could find some pictures of them. One time we re-enacted that down here, all the boys with their pick axes and old clothes and everything. It was Tom's birthday or something and we were putting on a show for him.

Q: A charade.

Streeter: Yes. Well, in any case, that's a side issue, but it was one of the things we did while the boys were growing up.

Then one summer, fairly soon after World War I (1925) when the American dollar was worth innumerable francs, we went to France. We went to Dinard, and we rented a little house in Dinard.

Q: The entire family?

Streeter: Well, yes, which was the three boys and Tom and me at this time. And this was the gate house to the Chateau that belonged to the Princess de la Tour d'Auvergne, I think, one of them. Anyhow, she was the sister of a friend of ours here. And it was a lovely little house. I have some pictures of these things somewhere, but it's hard to put my hand on them. And what charmed me entirely was that outside of the bedroom window, along the wall, was a lemon verbena vine, and that was just lovely. It's always been one of my favorite perfumes, and the bedroom was just filled with the perfume of lemon verbena.

Well, we had fun there.

Q: How long did you stay there?

Streeter: All summer, two months, I think. Because we got a French lady and her daughter. We employed them and they employed the household. I had taken over - well, you know, Cream of Wheat for the children and things like that, that they were used to.

Q: The indispensables.

Streeter: Right. Then we had trouble getting milk and cream. But there was one Englishwoman who ran a good dairy. They didn't pasteurize it in those days, and she got a young French boy on a bicycle to bring me cans over every morning. She sealed the cans every morning. She said, "Otherwise he will stop and take some milk and you will get yours watered."

So we had our problems, and they -

Q: I thought people were honest in those days.

Streeter: Well, the French can squeeze a penny, you know, if they have a chance. So, one time the cook was going to leave. I rented all the silver, all the china and everything. This was all part of the deal. So the cook told the French lady that she was going to leave, and the French lady said,

Streeter #3 - 136

"Very good, I myself am an excellent cook. I will be glad to cook for Madame Streeter." So the cook stayed.

Well, you can see. Tom and I had a lovely time. He wasn't over all the time. He was over about half the time. And we took <u>Mont St. Michel and Chartres</u>, by Henry Adams, and of course we were right near the Mont. St. Michel and we got to know that very well. We upset Madame Poularde terribly because we spent the night at her place - you know the rhyme, "John of Arc, with the aide of her lance drove the English out of France; Madame Poularde did better yet, she brought them back with her omelette."

Q: Did you get over to the Channel Islands?

Streeter: No, but we spent the night on the Mont. St. Michel, which is what you should do. Everybody else comes in the morning by train or bus. And goes back in the evening. You should spend the night, because then nobody is there but the people who live there; and we, Tom and I, we got a little sailboat and we sailed around the outside of the Mont, and it's from the ocean side that you see that wonderful "Mervielle," the wonderful stone wall with all the windows and all. So we spent some time there, and then we drove up along the coast, and we discovered a little church that Henry Adams wrote about, and which at that time the people in the neighborhood were paying no attention to. It was - well, you know "Chateau Fort" - it means it's a fort - this is what the church was, because they had the Vikings, it was way back in those days -- the Vikings would land. And you had no stained glass or anything else. You had a straight wall with clerestory windows. And all the neighbors would rush to the church and fort when the Vikings came.

Well, it was a ruin, of course. And we went to the little town, the name of which I forget at the moment, and we inquired everywhere for the church, and they sent us to every modern church in the village. We said, "This isn't what we're looking for." Finally we found somebody who told us --

Q: -- they thought you were looking for a place to pray.

Streeter: Right. We found the way out, and we were delighted with it. It was all overgrown at that time. Somebody was living in a little house near there, but nobody was taking much care of it. And since then they've made it of course a state monument, because it was very old. Henry Adams discovered it, and we discovered it, and now France has discovered it too.

Q: Yes, but the tourists hadn't begun to flock there in those days.

Streeter: No, and they hadn't known about this particular little church. So then of course we went to Chartres afterwards and Chartres was wonderful, but one of the things that interested me most. we went back after World War II to Chartres one time, when Tom and I were over, Henry Adams in hand, and they had taken down all the glass during World War II to avoid the bombing, and they washed it, and when they put it up again, as it must have been in the beginning, it just glittered. The first time we were there it was so dirty, after centuries of dust and all. It showed the lovely colors, but it didn't glow, the way it did after it was washed. We were impressed by it because we'd seen it before.

So we had a very pleasant summer, over there. This was all before Lil was born.

Well, then she was born - 1927.

Q: Did the boys have a tutor or anything during that time?

Streeter: They had a couple of nurses, I think. They were little, you see. They were three, five and seven, something like that.

Q: You didn't have anything for your family comparable to what your mother had for you when you were a child, a woman who - ?

Streeter: No. No. We had various ones that sort of came and went. Depending on what stage the children were at.

But this was before they were school age, you see.

So, let's see, where were some of the other places we went in the summer? We went up to the Adirondacks to Keene Valley, and when the children were little, we had houses in the valley (1929-32). But we did belong to the Ausable Club and we always loved to go into the lakes and camp out. That -

Q: - that was quite something to do in those days, was it not, to go to the Adirondacks?

Streeter: Oh, yes. Yes, indeed.

Q: Anybody, any person -

Streeter: Well, the 1890s was the big time for the Adirondacks, when you drove in by horse, and Mother had been there in that time. By the time we went, of course, you went by automobile.

But the Ausable Club was still going full tilt (1933-1937) good old 1890 architecture and very pleasant and very nice people, all of whom loved the woods - and there's a lower lake, that's about a mile and a half in, we used to have to drive up. Now they have a bus, but in the old days we had horse and wagon. Then, you have to row about two miles up the lower lake, which is long and narrow, and I've never ever, whether I was going in or coming out, been on the lower lake when the wind wasn't against me. Whether I was going up or going down. It turned around I suppose, it was always against me.

Then you walk for a mile along the Inlet, which is the river that runs between the upper lake and the lower lake. You get to the upper lake, and the upper lake had the cabins, the log cabins on it that are privately owned, but the rule is that you mustn't see the cabin from the lake. You see the dock where the canoes go in but not the cabins themselves.

So we went up there for several years, and Tom and I did a certain amount of mountain climbing.

Q: Riding horse back?

Streeter: No, on foot.

Q: But you did ride horse back also?

Streeter: No. No, you don't ride horse back in the Aidrondacks. You walk with a pack on your back, and you sleep in a lean-to when you get to the end of the day's walk. We had a wonderful old guide, Frank Wright. He was 70 years old, and he would carry twice the pack that we would carry. And I was not cut out for a mountain climber. But I huffed and I puffed and I got to the top of all the mountains

I could see. When I got up to the top of them once, I saw no point in going up a second time. I just said, "See that mountain? I've been on top of that mountain."

Q: But you did see the point in going up the first time.

Streeter: Oh, yes. Oh, yes. Then as the children got older of course they would come with us, and when they got older still they would climb the mountains.

The boys never took to it too much, but our daughter, by that time I'm talking about the 1930s, had come along, she loved the Adirondacks, and she's now bought one of the camps up there, and all her children and grandchildren come up there.

So I go up every once in a while to see her. And when I was finally in the Marine Corps in the early 1940s, and Tom and our daughter were the only ones at home, along came the summer time and I couldn't think where would be a good place for the two of them to go. We hadn't been to the Adirondacks for years I guess, by that time. And so I bethought me of the Ausable Club, because there are delightful older people for Tom to enjoy, and a great bunch of kids for Lil to enjoy. So they went up there two or three years and had a wonderful time.

Q: Did you have an opportunity to spend some time with them?

Streeter: No. I can't remember if I got up once. I'm not sure. I tried to get up once, but I think the rain was bad and I'm not sure I managed to make the flight.

Well, I'll tell you about that later, but I took very little of my leave while I was in the Marine Corps. I thought I might need it for something more important. If the boys were injured and it was possible to reach them, I wanted to have leave available.

Then, after I began to get out of breath in the Adirondacks, I said, "Now, children, next year we're going some place where you don't have to climb mountains."

So next time we went to Blue Hill, Maine. And for several summers we were in Blue Hill (1938-41) and that was great fun. The Seth Millikens, he was commodore of the yacht club there, and it was a nice group of teenagers by that time, and the children all loved it, and they're all good sailors. The two older boys went in the Navy. Tommy, the younger boy, went in the Army. He never was very keen about the sailing. But our daughter Lil is a very good sailor to this day. And Henry is a very good sailor. Frank wasn't so keen about it. I was a very poor sailor but I had a good time sailing.

I have found out that I really have had a lot of fun in the course of my life from doing the things I do badly. Now, this is unusual. Usually most people want to excel at what they do. Well, you always have to go through an awkward stage, and some things I did like mountain climbing and sailing, I never got out of the awkward stage. But if I'd said, "Oh, no, I can't do them," I would have missed an awful lot of fun. So I've enjoyed that.

Q: This says that you have some humility in your makeup.

Streeter: No - well, I don't think most people would agree with you.

Q: If you get a lot of fun out of things that you don't excel in.

Streeter: That's not humility, that's just a sense of humor.

Q: All right.

Streeter: Well, anyway, you can see we went along. I'm covering by leaps and bounds about twenty years in here, the 1920s and 1930s, and I'm afraid I'm going back and forth. Amont other things, we took the children West a number of times, and I get mixed up, because one year I took Henry and Frank, and another year I took Henry and Tommy, another year I took Tommy and Lil - I get a little mixed up as to when --

Q: Was there any design in these trips? Other than just pleasure or - ?

Streeter: Well, you see, on account of my grandfather, we'd had an interest in the West for years, the development of the West. I got them all to the Grand Canyon, and we usually would spend a couple of weeks on a ranch somewhere, you see, and then drive around the rest of the time. And I would write letters back to Tom and the children would write letters back to Tom, and when we got back he said, "I'm not at all sure you went on the same trip, your letters aren't on the same occasions — "

Q: Did he go with you on any of these?

Streeter: No. You see, he would stay here in the summer. We kept the big house open and it was nice and cool. He would stay here and we would go off one month, say July, and then he'd come to wherever we were in August, if we went on these trips.

Q: But he took only one month.

Streeter: Yes. He had to work. As we used to say — did I tell you about the way the children used to see him off in the morning, when they were little? We had a dining room and it had a big window, you see, and the car would come and pick him up about 7:45, take him to the train, and we and the police dog — we always had a police dog in those days - would all crowd around the window, "Yoo hoo," you know, and the question always was, "Where's Daddy gone?"

"Daddy's gone to get the bacon, bring the bacon home."

Q: In a chauffeur driven car.

Streeter: Yes, mostly a model T in the early days, sometimes better as time went on.

Well, into the midst of this happy family of course arrived the great Depression, and I don't think that I have really said very much about that.

Q: No, you haven't.

Streeter: Well, of course, one historical phase of my life was World War I. Another was the Great Depression. And it was because of the Great Depression largely that I got into this social work, if you want to call it, relief work.

Q: Yes, there was a crying need for that.

Streeter: A crying need. And the difference of course between then and now was that a great many men who had always been self-respecting, always earned their own way, always supported their own family, always taken pride in their work and in doing it well, lost their jobs - they didn't lose their jobs, the jobs simply vanished. And they were out of work, and this got to be very very bad, and Tom was out of work for a while. Then he was fortunate enough to get another job, and that was very helpful certainly to us, because you just had no money.

Q: You told me about him getting a job liquidating banks.

Streeter: Yes.

Q: Did it touch your own fortune, however, this Depression?

Streeter: Of course it did! Where do you think our fortune went? Nobody had any fortune left after the Great Depression. No. It went. It vanished like the jobs.

Well, anyhow, after a while it began to turn the corner. Money disappeared. Now, this is something you don't realize, but money disappeared, and we got practically down to barter, in the people that I was dealing with on the State Relief Council.

And as for a dollar, if you had a dollar in cash, you really could get almost anything for it.

Q: Yes, I remember how traumatic it was when the banks were all closed.

Streeter: Yes.

Q: And I had just gotten my salary in cash, so I was —

Streeter: — yes, you were lucky —

Q: — people wanting to borrow and all that kind of thing.

Streeter: Well, they carried us on credit for a little while at that time, and they gave various — you know, the butcher, the baker, the candle stick maker. But I took the children down to the bank, with the sign "Closed," and I rubbed their noses on the glass door, and I said, "Now, that's to make you remember the day when the banks were closed." It was like the story of Benvenito Cellini and the salamander?

Q: What's that?

Streeter: You don't know it? Oh well, every family has stories they're brought up on. Well, when Benvenito was a small boy, he was sitting beside his father one night in front of the fire, and he was being a good little boy, not doing anything bad at all, and suddenly his father cuffed him on the ear and knocked him off his stool, and of course he howled and he said, "What did you do that for?"

And his father said, "You see that little lizard in the fire?"

He said, "Yes, what about it?"

His father said, "That is a salamander. And I just want you to remember always that you saw a salamander in the fire."

"So that's what I cuffed you for, so you'd remember."

So I applied this same treatment the day the banks closed.

Q: Did you take the children into New York to see the bread lines and the people selling apples on the street?

Streeter: No need of that. Well, it went on for a long time. Then the corner started to turn, and of course what turned the corner eventually was the munitions for World War II. Before we got in. That created any number of jobs.

Well, I haven't said very much about Lil all this time. The boys, by the way, they all went to St. Paul's School. They hadn't any choice about that because their father had been there and my father had been there, and so, to St. Paul's they went. But they all did very well at St. Paul's.

Q: I would think they might.

Streeter: And Tom was always very proud of himself, because he paid full tuition the whole time they were there, and when three of them were there at the same time, Dr. Drury offered him a scholarship and he said, "No, we'll save on something else but we'll pay tuition for the boys."

So that was that, and I eventually had a grandson there and I have a grandchild there now. I have a granddaughter there now.

Q: Oh, they take girls?

Streeter: They take girls now. Then Frank and Henry went on to Harvard. Frank was in the class of 1940. Henry was in the class of '42. And Tommy, who was named after his father, went to Dartmouth. The Streeters were all good Dartmouth men, and Tom's father a trustee of Dartmouth for many, many years, and Tom himself very active in Dartmouth affairs, and young Tom went to Dartmouth.

Mr. Hopkins, Ernest Hopkins, who was the president was a great family friend, wonderful guy, too.

Well, Frank had just graduated from Harvard when we got in the war. I might tell you about the family, the boys in the war now. We'll go into other aspects of it later. He graduated in the spring of 1940, and at that time, people knew it was pretty close. They didn't know just when. He learned to fly, thought he might go in the Air Force. By that time I had a plane and Frank was flying me up along Cape Cod, and we knew, we could see there was weather coming in, smokey southeaster as a matter of fact. We got up to

Plymouth, and we considered coming down in an abandoned air field in Plymouth. Frank had learned to fly just about ten miles away, and thought he knew the countryside well enough to get there. So we started off flying along a railroad track, known as "the iron compass," good thing to have if you get in a rainstorm --

Q: Yes, it was used quite extensively in those days, wasn't it?

Streeter: Well, anyhow, we were flying along this. Nothing to the right of us, nothing to the left of us but cranberry bogs, which are not recommended as landing fields, and finally we were down below the tops of the factory chimneys, about 100 feet up or so, and it was pouring cats and dogs.

I said, "Frank, are you sure you know the way to get to that field? Is there a road going straight to it?

"Well, no, Mother."

I said, "Well, there's a nice field off to our right. Suppose we sit down. It's a little wet." Young corn. Of course, and that's a plowed field. You don't land in a plowed field in the main if you can help it. But we couldn't help it so we landed in it, and he made a nice job of landing; but of course what happens is, your wheels stick in the mud, your tail comes up, and you land on your head. Broke the propeller but otherwise no damage done.

Q: What was this plane?

Streeter: My plane.

Q: Yes, but what kind?

Streeter: Oh, it was a Stinsom Voyager, 90 horsepower, single engine. Very nice plane. I flew it a lot.

So then, Frank had to get back to La Guardia, where he was working at that time, had a job at that time, and this was Sunday afternoon, so he hitched a ride up to Boston, and I sent up to Boston for somebody to come down and get the plane and tow it up. In the meantime of course I got absolutely soaking wet. Never was wetter in my life.

The farmer that owned the field was very hospitable, but he didn't have any fire. Not any fire in the house. No heat to dry me out at all. They had a kerosene stove to cook on.

So they said, "Well, tell you what, there's a steam laundry downtown, and if you go down there, they'll dry your things for you."

So I went down to the steam laundry and they found a convenient closet to tuck me into, while they took off my things and dried them out for me.

The farmer had a young daughter, and I gave the broken propeller to her for a souvenir. She wrote, when she saw I'd got in the Marines, she wrote me a letter. She remembered who I was.

We got the plane towed up to Boston, and had to leave it there for a couple of weeks to get repaired. Then I went up to get it. So I said to the aviation people, "Well, have you test flown it since you repaired it?"

"Oh no, lady, we don't test fly it, you test fly it."

I said, "All right, I'll go up and test fly it, but if I find any trouble, mind you, I'm going to come back and tweak your nose."

It was all right of course and I got it back again in good order. So if you want to know about my assorted experiences, these are some of them. I think some of that is in the Tales of An Ancient Mariner.

And I won't tell you all about what the boys did, because that's also in Tales Of An Ancient Mariner.

Q: Yes, and you have told me something about that.

Streeter: There was quite a lot about that. But that brings them up to the time of the war, and brings me pretty well up to the time of the war. But because my home life was so much, up to that time, the most important thing, I wanted to get that background out of the way.

You see, both before and after the war, I devoted only my spare time to these other things. Some times I had more spare time than others, I could do more.

Q: What do you mean by spare time? How much time would you be able to devote?

Streeter: I don't know. It varied. When the children were all home, of course I couldn't do very much. And when they began going off to boarding school and college, then of course I could do more. Even after Tom retired, which he did in '39, he was absorbed completely in his book collection, so that still left me with a good deal of spare time.

Q: You might give me a picture of your home life when the boys were still at home, or at school and coming back.

Streeter: Well, we had a great big rambling house, which was fine at that time because they could bring any friends home that they wanted to, and —

Q: — how big was this house? I know the location, but how big was it in those days?

Streeter: Well, it had three floors, plus a basement and an attic, and there were one, two, three, four, five, about five or six bedrooms, and downstairs there was the living room, which was a big room, and Tom's library which was an even bigger room, and a dining room of course and the maid's quarters.

Q: How many servants did you have then in the house?

Streeter: Well, I think we had three generally. We had a cook and a waitress and a chambermaid. And then if we had anybody with the children, a nurse, that would be another one. And usually, sometimes one of them was part of a couple, and the man would drive Tom around, to the train and all and meet him, and also keep up the grounds.

Q: You mentioned in passing, putting on a show for some family celebration, a show of life in the Klondike or something of the sort. Was this a family custom, to have plays within the family for occasions?

Streeter: Oh, not as formal as that. We just had sort of "Oh Be Joyful" occasions every once in a while.

Q: Who organized them?

Streeter: I don't know. It was spontaneous. And of course, after the house burned down partially, we were firemen for a long time. The boys were. That was before Lil was born.

Q: Did you have reading sessions or anything of that sort in the family? Would Mr. Streeter read out loud to the children?

Streeter: Well, no, but I did. That sofa you're sitting on, this is when they were quite little, I would curl up on that end, you see, and between me and the back was what was known as the "cubby hole", and the smallest child got the cubby hole. They'd have their supper at six. We wouldn't have ours till seven. So between supper time and the time that Tom got back from New York, I would read to them in the evening. As I say, they all sat around and the smallest child got in the cubby hole.

Q: What sort of thing did you read to them?

Streeter: Well, a lot of it was sort of nonsense, but they were mostly fairy tales and things like that, because when they got beyond the fairy tale stage, they could read themselves.

Q: Were they avid readers?

Streeter: Yes, they all liked to read. All of them. Intelligent. Henry and Lil, when they were in school, along about thirteen or so, were the top ones in the testing thing in the country, I think. There was a testing thing. The top one got 100 and the others got marks in relation to that.

Q: For reading comprehension?

Streeter: Yes. They were not subject tests but the intelligence tests. So they both did well on that, and the others did well too.

Q: Were they interested in your husband's collection of rare books?

Streeter: Well, Tom didn't collect very much until after the Depression.

Q: I see.

Streeter: And after he retired. He had been in and out of the collecting business. He collected - he had to learn, of course, because he got stung a few times. Auctions are very insidious things to go to. And then, he began to know more about it. To begin with he got sort of like Old Masters, I mean well known and expensive books. Those went by the wayside fairly early, because his real interest was in Americana, the discovery of America and the first books in all the 48 states, and he had this wonderful collection; and I bought out this book which you can take home with you if you like. I can show you his catalogue, which is in seven volumes. This is Bookman's Yearbook, it reprinted the very nice article that Lawrence Wroth wrote about Tom, which is the introduction to his catalogue, and then there are articles from various other dealers and friends too. You might like to look at it. But it really was not until after he retired that he could devote himself to his books.

When he finished up one of these jobs of settling a bank that had got in trouble, and he'd wrung out as much money as he could for the people who had lost their money in it, and this was the end of '39, he came home one day and he said, "I don't want to stay with this job. We've got everything but the pennies now, and it's hardly worth sticking with it that long; and I'd rather not go looking for another job, and I think I've learned enough about investments and all to become" - I guess more cautious he said, "I think I can support us."

Q: You mean, '29 had taught him a lesson?

Streeter: Oh, he never borrowed money after '29. This of course was what ruined everybody, was margin sales.

He said, "I think what I'd really like to do is retire." He was 57 at the time. "And really devote myself to my book collection, and I've always been an historian at heart, and this is what I'm really interested in. How about it?"

I said, "I think that's fine. Go right ahead." And so he had a whole second career. The first 25 years of our marriage, you see, he was working; and then the last 25 years he was retired and was collecting his books.

People would say to me, "Isn't it nice your husband's got a hobby now that he's retired?" and I'd say, "Hobby? You don't know. This is a big business. He's got a librarian and a secretary and he's constantly writing letters and on the telephone. This is very professionally done, I'll have you know."

So, in the end - oh, he was on all kinds of committees, a friend of pretty nearly every library in the country, I guess. I don't mean the ordinary libraries but the rare book libraries. And he was president of the Antiquarian Society. He was president of the Grolier Club. He was president of, I don't know what, and he was a member of the Walpole Club, which as a matter of fact our two older sons are members of now, too.

And so he really had a whole new life for 25 years, and just exactly what he wanted to do, which I think is fine.

Well, he decided, and he told all his book collector friends about this, that he was going to have it sold at auction after his death. That he'd had so much fun collecting books that he'd like other people to have fun, instead of leaving it all in one place.

But before he did that, he began with the history of Texas, up to 1840, up to the time it became a republic, and up to the Mexican War, and that was because when he was in oil, he used to go to Texas, and somewhat to Mexico. I went with him once or twice down to the Texas oilfields when they were new. Boy, were they a mess.

Q: Which fields did you visit?

Streeter: Oh, I couldn't tell you now, I've forgotten, but they were pretty new at the time, and —

Q: — a pretty rugged life.

Streeter: Yes. That was how he got his first interest in Texas. Then of course he was very much interested in it because it was an interesting place, and he gave his Texas collection to Yale, as a collection, because it fitted in with other collections there. There were Wagner's Collection, Wagner was a great collector out in California, and I think there was one other — the Coe Collection. So that is down at Yale, the Streeter Collection on Texas. But the rest were just about all auctioned.

He died in '65, and of course it took a little time to get everything appraised. He had catalogued it himself, in something like 87 little black books, and written notes on each one — this of course took him years. He had screened it himself, because he was always particular — he'd get a bundle of books, of course, and there would be one that was really awfully good and the rest were second rate, or at least didn't fit his collection. He gave away for instance a lot of railroad books to people who were interested in that, and other ones that were not along the main line of his interest.

And so, in due time, he had reduced his collection to something like 5,000 books, the ones he kept. And the book dealers and the book collectors would come out here and I'd put them up and give them a good dinner and all that, and got to know them of course very well.

But I always said I didn't know anything about the books, because if you're going to know anything about rare books, you've got to either know all about them or nothing about them. There's no use having a smattering about rare books. This was not my line at all. I'm sure that Tom didn't want it to be my line. This was _his_ turf. So he was very much absorbed in it.

After his death they took his notebooks, Parke-Bernet did, and they didn't use his notes entirely, but it was the basis for most of their notes, and I'll show you the catalogues there.

Q: What role did you play in the liquidation of the collection?

Streeter: I was an executor. Tom had suggested three men that we knew very well, Mike Walsh and Ed Eberstadt and one other as an advisory board, and Doc O'Conner, who was an old friend of his –

Q: Is that Basil O'Connor?

Streeter: Basil O'Connor. He'd been in Tom's law office in Boston, and Tom had encouraged him to come over to New York. And darned if he didn't turn up as the law partner of Franklin Roosevelt!

Q: It brought him all sorts of good things.

Streeter: So, that was very nice. So Doc and I were the two executors, and we used to come and sit around the table, you know, and talk about this and that with the consultants.

Every once in a while, a book would come up, and they'd talk about it. I'd ask about it and then I'd tell them what ought to be done about it. They'd say, "Huh? Where did you know about that book?"

I said, "I lived with these books for 25 years, I must have known something about it." I just didn't pretend to know everything about it.

So it took seven auctions. There were two auctions a year. We got the books out of the big house in March of '66. Then I moved over here right afterwards. I couldn't stay in that big house all by myself. I couldn't leave until the books were out. They were in a fireproof vault with a safe door on it. I had the key and the combination to it. They finally got all moved to New York, and then I guess it was the autumn of '66, was the first sale. It's all out there anyhow. They had seven of them. And they went very well. I think they grossed $3,100,000 or something like that.

Well, the net of course was much less. You had taxes and you had Parke-Bernet's fee and you had legal fees and – but it was still –

Q: – a considerable amount.

Streeter: An amount. And at the time it set a record for books. But now that, you see, was the end of, began in '66, it was 3½ years; it was getting on to 1970, and by that time, we were beginning to get a lot of inflation. And now, those things, objets d'art and all, are bringing huge prices.

Q: Incredible amounts.

Streeter: Very inflated prices. And we had about forty books, I think, which were known in the family as the "Crown Jewels." They were special ones. And one of them, oh dear, I can't remember all these things now, but one of them was the Cambridge Platform.

Q: Cambridge Platform?

Streeter: Yes. The Cambridge Platform was the second book published in Massachusetts. The first book was the Bay Psalm Book. And Yale got that.

The Cambridge Platform was a platform of church discipline, and that was the second book; and there were many of these books, you see, that Tom had the last copy of. They would have been given to some library and therefore sterilized, you see, and Tom had the only copy —

Q: — that was still in a private collection, you mean.

Streeter: Right. And in the depths of the Depression, I always gave him great credit for this, he sold some of his best books. I mean, you asked what happened to our fortune — it went and he sold The Cambridge Platform, and that must have been a heartbreaker really for him.

I don't know, five or six years afterwards, we were having dinner one night and he said, "Oh, by the way, there's an interesting auction going on in New York tonight."

I said, "So? What's in it?"

He said, "Well, The Cambridge Platform is in it, my copy of The Cambridge Platform."

I said, "Good gracious, Tom, don't you want to go in?"

"Oh, no," he said, "I want to stay away from it. But I've put in a bid for it." And he did get it back again.

Q: Oh, he got it back again?

Streeter: Yes. His own copy. And after his death it was sold at auction for $80,000. Mike Walsh had been told - did you ever know Mike? Goodspeeds. Mike was the head of this section in Goodspeeds, wonderful guy, and many times out here. I think he was the one Tom depended on most.

So Mike was sent over by Harvard with, something like a 40, or 50 thousand dollar bid. So they kept going up, and Mike kept going up. Finally he got it at $80,000.

So our son Henry who lives in Boston saw Mike on the street the next day and said, "Well, Mike, how did you get along?"

He said, "I got The Cambridge Platform."

Henry said, "Oh yes, but you paid $80,000 for it."

"Oh, yes," said Mike, "I guess so."

Henry said, "What are you going to do?"

Mike said, "Pass the hat."

Henry said, "What are you going to do if nobody fills up the hat?"

Mike said, "Go back to Ireland."

And then there was the Pigaffetta.

Q: Would you talk a little about it?

Streeter: Pigaffetta was a young man of good family, and he went - paid his way to be a passenger on the trip of Magellan around the world, and he kept a diary, and this is his diary.

Q: I see.

Streeter: It was published on his return in various languages, but this was really the original one. Did I tell you the story about our daughter going to Machu Pichu? It had to do with the Pigaffetta.

Well, I'm wandering all over the lot -

Q: That's all right.

Streeter: This is sort of local color. Well, she and her son and his wife were traveling in South America, I guess about five years ago, and they took the railroad train up to Machu Pichu, which is the ruins of the Inca city in the Andes.

Q: Parallels the Urubamba River.

Streeter: It's on the top of a mountain.

Q: Yes, I've been on that railroad.

Streeter: You have? Well, the cars weren't crowded, and there were two nice gentlemen who seemed to be having an interesting time and were pleasant appearing, and they struck up an acquaintance, and they asked Lil and her son if they'd been having a nice time in South America. Lil said yes, they had, but they were disappointed that they hadn't had time enough to go round the Horn, as Magellan did.

So then they got discussing Magellan, and these two gentlemen smiled sweetly and said - well, one turned out to be a professor at whichever university it is, Minnesota, I think, and the other was the rare book librarian, and they said, "Well, you would be interested to know that we have in our library the Pigaffetta, and some time when you're out in the neighborhood, come and see it."

And Lil smiled twice as sweetly and she said, "Oh, yes, I know the Pigaffetta. You have my father's copy."

There in the middle of the Andes, they run across Magellan!

Well, you know, things like that are always happening. It makes for an interesting life.

Q: Tell me about the kind of entertaining you did when you had the big house and the family.

Streeter: Well, it was part of our life. I mean, you just did it as part of your life.

Q: Dinner parties or what?

Streeter: Oh, yes. Dinner parties. One time my husband

said to me, "Ruth, why do we always have to have flaming peaches when people come here for dessert?"

I said, "Why, Tom, that's because they like flaming peaches and that's why they come to dinner."

Q: They're also spectacular.

Streeter: Yes. Very good too. You have to learn how to make them flame, too, because you can poor on brandy and brandy but if you don't get it hot enough, it won't flame.

Q: How many would you have for a dinner party?

Streeter: Oh, usually eight. Eight is a good number, if you can manage –

Q: How formal or informal were the dinner parties?

Streeter: Rather formal.

Q: Dress up affairs.

Streeter: Yes. The men would wear tuxedoes. We didn't have white tie things very much. Black tie. Ladies in evening dress.

Q: And then a division after dinner?

Streeter: Oh, yes. Tom would take them off into his library. And then there was another - it says in these books here, these articles about him, that he had a shelf particularly for the ladies, because they would come out later, but they didn't know a thing about it, you know, so he'd have some Kipling, Balzac - he'd have some books by people that they would have heard of, and those were the ones he called his "Oh My" books. "Oh, my, you've got something like that?" They didn't really know what it was all about.

Oh, yes, we did that sort of thing. It was part of your life.

Q: What did your friends tend to be? Professional people or business people?

Streeter: They were people who lived out here, mostly, and you know, worked in New York. And then of course the children's friends, from school and college and all that. It was a nice group. But of course, there aren't so many of them left, now.

Q: We're going to talk about your Civil Air Patrol career, which was not very long, but you were bound and determined to make some contribution, when we were getting into war, so you decided to learn to fly. Tell me about that?

Streeter: Well, I suppose that this was largely because of my younger brother, interested in flying, and –

Q: – and the yearly awards that were given in his memory.

Streeter: Yes. That's right. And it was obvious by this time, by 1940, after the fall of France, that we were certainly likely to be drawn into the war in Europe. Of course, we had three boys of just the age that would be going in, and this was pretty upsetting to anybody of my generation, because we thought we had fought "the war to end war" and here it was our own sons just coming up the right age to go into another one.

Much of my feeling about all this, and about what the boys did and about my flying, is in the little privately published book called Tales Of An Ancient Mariner, so I won't go into too much detail about it, but I will say that I started to fly in a J-3 Cub. A J-3 Cub is single motor, 75 horsepower. It's about the smallest thing that will fly, I think.

Q: Where did you take instruction?

Streeter: Over here, the air field in Caldwell, New Jersey.
Well, I got to enjoy flying. I was scared most of the time I flew, but that's part of the game. I don't think

you ever get to the point of being bored flying. I imagine it's rather like riding to hounds, a little element of danger to it adds to the zest, and also it's a game, because as you get better and better at it, you're less and less likely to pile up.

Q: What was your husband's attitude about this?

Streeter: I didn't even tell him about this until I'd got my license, I think.

Q: Oh, you did not?

Streeter: No.

Q: How did he react when he learned of it?

Streeter: Well, he was a little surprised, but I guess he'd got over being surprised at me by that time. You know. Things were looking kind of bad so he didn't try to object to it at all.

Well, I did get my private pilot's license, and then I kept on until I got a commercial pilot's license.

Q: How long did it take you, this course of training?

Streeter: I began, I suppose, in '40, 1940. After all Pearl Harbor was in December of '41, so I suppose it's about a year and a half before, something like that.

Q: And one of your sons was becoming a pilot simultaneously.

Streeter: That's right. That was in the summer of '41. And by that time, I had bought my own little plane and I'd joined the Civil Air Patrol, and this was a very frustrating experience because after Pearl Harbor, the Civil Air Patrol was allowed to fly off of Atlantic City in March, worst weather of the year of course, in single motored land planes - something that nobody in their right mind would do unless there was a particular overriding reason for it.

Q: The overriding reason was the German submarines.

Streeter: German submarines were sinking our ships in plain sight of Atlantic City, a mile or two offshore, and they wouldn't even torpedo them. They surfaced and shot them down with deck guns. And by having some sort of air cover, which probably looked more important than it was if you saw it through a periscope, we succeeded reasonably well in keeping them down. It was flown by my squadron, of which I was adjutant, for amonth or six weeks.

They wouldn't let me fly. I was of course absolutely furious.

Q: You were adjutant, but –

Streeter: I was adjutant of it. In other words, I did all the dirty work.

Q: You mean you organized the schedules and everything.

Streeter: Yes. I mean, whatever there was. There's always the commanding officer and he passes the word along to the exec, and the exec passes it on to the adjutant, so there you are.

Q: How many fliers were engaged in this?

Streeter: Well, I can't tell you very much about it, because I was so mad I wouldn't even go down.

Q: Were there other women?

Streeter: No. They wouldn't let the women fly. I don't think there were any other women in the squadron, not as pilots anyhow.

Q: I see. You were the sole woman.

Streeter: They picked on me. And I didn't appreciate it at all. In fact, I was very much disappointed, of course.

They did a very good job, and I did let them have my plane. Two of the men in the squadron flew my plane down there.

Q: Did they carry bombs or anything of the sort?

Streeter: Yes, they had a 100 pound bomb tied on with a piece of chickenwire, I think.

Q: A single bomb.

Streeter: Or picture wire. Yes. As far as I know they never dropped it.

This was a sort of a Dunkirk type of thing, you know. And they had small boats there, too, to help pick anybody up, if they could find anybody to pick up. It was, I think it was well worthwhile, and later it was better organized, better equipped, and flown all up and down the Atlantic Seaboard.

Q: Now, this was under the aegis of what, Navy?

Streeter: The Civil Air Patrol.

Q: Under the Army?

Streeter: It was under the Navy here, and that was our

trouble, because we had a sort of a cookie-pusher admiral, who was admiral of the sea frontier off New York, and he wouldn't let any boats or planes fly for months unless they were Navy boats and planes. And of course the Navy had other things to do with its boats and planes.

Q: Who was that, Andrews?

Streeter: Yes, Admiral Adolphus Andrews. We didn't think much of him. But then by March we'd worn him down a little and he let us do what we could. Also, I think he was relieved, presently.

Q: Retired about that time, I think. Well, tell me a little more about the training itself, when you were acquiring your license.

Streeter: Well, the training is very good. You move from step to step. I was always, as a matter of fact, a better flier than I was a sailor, because I just picked up sailing, and I was 35 years old when I was learning to sail and that's too old. You should pick up sailing when you're a child.

I was taught flying step by step, the way you're taught anything, if you have a proper teacher, and I was 47 by that time, and I just moved on from one step to another, and there are various kinds of exercises you have to do.

Q: Did you acquire any knowledge about mechanics? Looking after the engine, that sort of thing?

Streeter: Yes. I wouldn't say I could take it apart, but I had to pass an exam on what the different functions of the various parts of the engine were. And you always, if you were sensible, looked your engine over before you took off. A little inclined to find dirt in the gasoline tank, things like that.

Q: Did you have any close calls during this training period?

Streeter: Yes. There's quite a lot of this in Tales Of An Ancient Mariner so I don't want to do too much of it. I made at least three forced landings, one of them was the one that my son made –

Q: That is included in the Tales –

Streeter: Yes. I made two others. And also, there are all the ones I didn't make, which is important too, because I started to fly with a – I took several cross country flights with more experienced pilots, just so as to learn about navigation, learn about flying conditions.

Q: Across the state?

Streeter: No. I went down to Florida and I went out as far as Omaha. One time. You know, you've got to learn to find your way, and of course, I always keep one foot on the ground, more or less, as you might say, because in the first place my plane wouldn't go above 8,000 feet, and in the second place, I will say that I navigated largely by looking at the terrain, especially if I had any handy railroad tracks going where I wanted to go.

Q: Were you equipped with Rand McNally road maps?

Streeter: Well, to begin with, I had airplane maps, which of course are better for flying. But in the end they impounded all those, and I did have road maps, when I went out to Omaha.

But when you get between the Alleghenies and the Rockies, it's flat anyhow and it's not so hard to see where you're going. Also the weather's likely to be better, although we have thunder storms and things.

Well, one time we started to fly, a pilot from my squadron and I, from here to Louisville, Kentucky, and this was a wonderful time. We got over the - what's the name of these mountains here?

Q: The Alleghenies?

Streeter: The Alleghenies, yes - and they are like wrinkles on your hand, there's a ridge, then a valley, then a ridge and a valley, and you go off across them, which works better some times than others.

We got to the next to the last valley. We only had one more ridge to go, and the weather was closing in. Couldn't see the top of the ridge that we had to get over to get to the next airport. So I suggested to the pilot that we go up into the clouds and count ten and come down on the other side.

He said, "Oh, no, we won't. In the first place neither of us are blind fliers. We'll be upside down before we know it. And we don't know how long it will take us to get over the next ridge and we're liable to hit it."

Well, by that time the clouds had settled down on the ridge behind us too. So we flew up and down the valley until we found a nice wheat field and we landed in the wheat field.

Then we spent a little time in the wheat field. I think we spent two days in that valley, before the weather was good enough for us to take off again.

But they flew the mail across the Alleghenies. When was this? '42. And the way they flew the mail past these little mountain towns, they had two big poles up with a wire between them and the mail bag attached to the wire, and the mail plane came along with a great hook, and just hooked it up, you see, and winched it up into the plane. There was no place for them to land.

So presently the plane came through from Pittsburgh. So we said, well, if it's going to come through from Pittsburgh we can go back to Pittsburgh, so we lit out of the valley and we flew the passes and we got into Pittsburgh.

Nobody had noticed that we had been sitting on the ground for two days, although we had filed a flight plan!

Then from Pittsburgh we took off and we were going to an air meet in Louisville, Kentucky. We got as far as Cincinnati and we started off on what we thought was the last lap to Louisville, and the thunderstorms kept forming. You can see thunderstorms form, if your humidity and temperature get within a certain distance of each other. So there was one formed to the right. That was all right, we just flew off to the left. Then there was another formed to the left, but we still thought we'd go between them, till one formed right in front of us, and we didn't want to go back, so we picked a good looking field and we sat down in it.

And no sooner had we sat down in it than a bunch of policemen in a jeep came up to us. We found it was the field belonging to the women's reformatory, prison, and they wanted to know what in heaven's name we were doing on their front lawn?

We said we didn't know it was your front lawn, it was the best looking front lawn around, so we sat down on that.

We stayed the night. And of course by the time we got to Louisville, the meet was all over. They'd all gone home.

Q: But in flying you always avoided thunderstorms.

Streeter: Well, yes. We avoided several things. Then one time I flew down to Florida, to visit some friends of mine down there, and we saw a thunderstorm coming up, and the road went off on a triangle, you see - I mean, on two sides of a triangle, and you could go direct into Jacksonville by a shorter route, if you flew over the swamps.

So I was still flying with a more experienced flier, which is an excellent way to learn, and I said, "Oh well, why do we follow the road? Why don't we get ahead of this thing and go down straight to Jacksonville?"

He said, "Lady, will you look at that swamp?"

One of these, you know, the stream was zig zagging and meandering all through it, and the rest of it was nothing but mud, and he said, "You go down in here, nobody's ever going to find you, ever. They won't ever find you and they won't ever be able to get you out of there."

Q: Except the alligators.

Streeter: Except the alligators. He said, "Lady, you stick to the road." So I stuck to the road. It's just as well.

Because of course we ran straight into the thunderstorm, and by this time, it was blowing so hard that we were flying sideways down the road, in order to get to Jacksonville. You couldn't fly striaght down - the wind pushed us across, so we went this way down the road, about, I don't know, not more than about 80 feet up, I guess, to the great entertainment of all the people in the automobiles.

Well, I learned another thing - never fly over swamps if you can fly anywhere else. And you learn about those things. Then you get off by yourself, and you put what you've learned into practice.

Q: What sort of instrumentation did you have?

Streeter: Nothing except we had an altimeter, speedometer, a rate of climb meter, we had a compass and we had a bank and turn thing, that's all. But I had a special kind of compass. It didn't swing as much as they ordinarily do. I prided myself on that.

Q: Was this open cockpit?

Streeter: No. No. But it's much better, if you've got rain and things like that, in winter time and all. I did learn to fly a float plane too. And then I learned to fly a lovely thing called a UPF-7, and that was fun. That was open cockpit, and you know, you had a helmet and all those things and you felt you were really flying. That was a biplane. Sometimes known as the Yellow Peril.

That was a good plane. I liked it. Well, I think that's about enough.

Q: You had thought that you would be able to ferry planes.

Streeter: Yes. Get into the WASPS. The WASPS were the Women's Air Service Pilots. And I had thought of that right along, because the English women were flying planes in England, and in fact, one of the girls that flew at the same field that I did was secretary to Jackie Cochran, and she later went over to fly in England. I had thought that the women would get organized as ferry pilots, and sure enough, they did. But by that time I was 47, and 35 was the age limit.

Q: 35 was the limit?

Streeter: 35 was the age limit. So I got thrown out by everybody about four times. Finally I got to see Jackie Cochran herself and got thrown out the fifth time.

I explained, younger people would be likely to wash out, and here I was already with most of my pilot's licenses. I had a commercial pilot's license by that time. I was in the midst of a blind flying course. And why didn't they take me, that they already had half trained? Because I knew of course a number of these girls by this time.

Jackie was in charge of the training. But then she was not in charge of them after they were trained. A girl named Nancy Love was more or less in charge of them. But they never had a definite status, such as the women in the Army, Navy and Marine Corps had. They were sort of auxiliaries, and they never got treatment as veterans until just this last year, about a month ago.

Q: Yes, I know, it took years of agitation in order to do it.

Streeter: Yes, and this really was not fair. They got a simulated rank of second lieutenant, pay of second lieutenant, and I suppose maybe got promoted - I think there were about a thousand of them in the end. I lost track of them, after I finally found I wasn't going to be able to get in, because I gave up that idea. But I know that they did do a good job. And I couldn't blame Jackie Cochran for not taking me, because after I got in the Marine Corps, people would apply that had good qualifications but again they were over the age limit. We might I suppose have waived - got them a waiver if they'd had some very, very special skill, but by law we were limited to -

Q: — and waivers are discriminatory.

Streeter: Yes. So as I say, I was disappointed but I couldn't exactly hold her responsible for it.

Q: You make a very interesting point, as I remember, in the Tales, and that is that you were scared to death very often when you were flying, but this didn't negate the fact that you had your wits about you.

Streeter: Well, this I think is very important, and I put that in for the sake of my grandchildren, because being scared is different from being panicky. When you're panicky you just, you know, all shaking, can't think what to do. If you're scared, you can still think. As I say, it's not a very pleasant sensation, but it's what all of these men must have that have been getting the Cheney Award. And it's what all experienced soldiers have, as distinguished from the green recruits.

Q: You mean it's acquired?

Streeter: Oh, it's an acquired thing. Absolutely acquired. And it's acquired by repetition.

Q: There's a basic confidence you have in your skill, your ability.

Streeter: Well, or a fatalism, or whatever you want to call it. I don't know what they've done in some other services but I know the Marines, when they really had gotten the men along in their training, they fired live ammunition over them while they crawled under barbed wire fences. Now, I think there must be a point somewhere, but this I wouldn't know, where you had too much; and this is when people get battle fatigue and all that. There must be a point at which you can't take it any more. But for a long time, depending I suppose more or less on temperament, and on training, it's training, training - you can go on.

I think, that's what they're going to find out when they put women into combat.

Q: That was a very interesting lesson you learned.

Streeter: Oh, yes. Well, a lot of other people have learned it, too.

Q: Yes. Were there other observations that you acquired from this experience as a flier?

Streeter: Well, I don't know. As I say, I never really finished that. Most of my observations have been frustrated. But I remembered how my brother used to love being up in the air, and this is so. You have, in those days, you have a wonderful sense of freedom. I don't know that you have now, because you have to listen to your radio all the time, and you have to listen to all your instructions when you're coming into a field or taking off from a field. There's an awful lot of sky, and it's fun to be up in it and to look all around. Of course, the earth is foreshortened, and it does terrible things to mountains. You should always look up to mountains. You shouldn't look down on mountains. They're all foreshortened. It doesn't treat them right. That's not the way they're meant to be looked at.

Of course, I fly a lot in planes, commercial planes. You're up 40, 50 thousand feet and it's zero outside or something but you don't know it. Flying the sort of little plane that I flew is like sailing a little boat. Entirely different from getting on the Queen Elizabeth II or something like that.

You're much more in touch with the air, and you begin to have a very great respect for the weather. Sailing and flying are very much alike. You have to allow for your winds and your weather the way you do in both of them, except that things happen much quicker in a plane.

Q: How long did you continue to fly?

Streeter: I gave it up when I went into the Marine Corps.

Q: You gave it up completely?

Streeter: Yes, they wouldn't let me fly.

Q: And you've never flown since?

Streeter: Well, I think I took one weekend off and flew when I was in the Marine Corps. But I'd sold my plane to the Civil Air Patrol, and I obviously wasn't going to be allowed to fly. I said to General Waller, "I have a weekend off and I haven't flown for a long time. I don't want to lose my skill entirely, and there's a little place along the railroad there where I could go."

Of course we had gas rationing. I couldn't go by car. And walk up to where this little field was. "Would you have any objection if I went off Saturday and Sunday?" It was a weekend. I had leave.

And he said, "No, why should I?"

I said, "You spent a lot of time breaking me into this job. Maybe you wouldn't like it if I broke my neck."

He said, "Why should I care? The Marine Corps is set up to take care of people that break their necks. Go ahead."

So I went out to this place. I don't know that this really belongs in here —

Q: Sure.

Streeter: Want me to tell stories? Well, they're true stories, anyhow. I went out to this place, lugging my little bag, up a sandy road to a farmhouse where I was going to spend the night. There was the daughter of a Navy officer, nice youngster, and she was doing the same thing I was, going to spend the night in the same place, so we went up to this field, which was nothing but a little, you know, field, a meadow. Got a plane. Not much of a plane. I've forgotten what it was. But I just practiced landings pretty much, take offs and landings. I didn't look around the countryside very much. But when I got up there one day, there was a considerably larger plane, I've forgotten what kind it was now, but it was orange and black, and there was a man and woman who were flying that, and they were going to fly over to a club, a flying club which was twenty miles or so away. So the kid who was with me, she couldn't get a plane, they were all busy, so they said, "Well, would you like to fly over with us? We're going over and you can find your own way back." So she did. And she came back and spent the night in the same place I was.

I said, "What was the flight like?"

She said, "Oh, they were both just as drunk as they could be." She said, "I was never so glad to get down on the ground again. I had to hitchhike my way back and I'm very glad to be out of it."

So the next morning I was flying around a little wider space, so I thought, I'll fly over and take a look at this place.

There was the orange and black plane, in bits, at this private airport. I went down to find out what had happened, and sure enough, they must have been tight as ticks, and the two men took off after lunch when they probably had more to drink, and they cracked up. Both killed.

Q: You mean, the man and woman?

Streeter: No, the woman didn't go up with them. He met some pal there. And he and this pal went up and they crashed, spun in, and were both killed.

Q: What would induce people to fly when they're tight?

Streeter: I don't know. What induces people when they're tight to do all kinds of things?

Well, anyhow, that was my only experience with flying after I got in the Marine Corps. I had plenty of other things to do, I couldn't spare the time.

Q: That was your last experience in flying?

Streeter: Well, it didn't do me any harm, but it certainly showed what can happen.

I think, as I say, I was frustrated. I spent a lot of time and effort on this (1940-42). I was sorry that I couldn't make it do something really useful. But when it was evident that I wasn't going to be allowed to do anything useful, I sat down to look around to see what else I could do.

Q: There was a certain sense of achievement. You had learned to fly.

Streeter: What good did that do me? That wasn't why I learned it. Oh, I was quite upset about it, but I just had to sit down and think what the next possibility would be.

And that's when the Marine Corps came along and solved my problem. Ask me questions if they occur to you.

Q: Yes. We're about to turn to the chapter that deals with the Marine Corps. Now, you had a statement to make. At the beginning of this chapter.

Streeter: Well, this is to request your indulgence, because the method of an oral history is rather new to me, and not one with which I'm entirely familiar. I belong to the generation that read and then wrote. And if I sit down to write something, which I can work over several times, and look back and see what I said before, it makes sense and holds together. But, by this time I've forgotten what I've put in and what I left out, in most of my previous remarks, and there may be duplications, and they may not hold together as well as they otherwise would.

Q: Let me add my little note and say, they all make sense.

Streeter: Well, if you have a good time listening to them, that is part of the game.

Q: I think we're coming to the end of the tape so I'll turn it over.

You were telling about the first notice that came to you, the fact that you were being considered for this job as Director of the lady Marines. This came about in 1942, I believe, when Basil O'Connor had lunch with your husband.

Streeter: It was in January of '43, I think, and up to this time, none of us knew that the Marines were even considering taking women. I was feeling very low in my mind, at not having been able to do anything along the line of flying, which I had spent some time acquiring a certain facility in, and I was looking for something that would be really useful to do.

Q: Did you have anything specific in mind that you were looking for?

Streeter: Well, I had been down to the WAVES and asked them if they let women fly and they said they didn't. And I might apply if I wanted to be a ground instructor. It said, I didn't want to be. I said I already had a commercial pilot's license. I want to fly.

So I didn't get very far with the WAVES. Therefore, I was still up in the air, as you might say, wondering what to do next.

Q: Did you approach the Army?

Streeter: Not really seriously, and the Coast Guard, I had not been to. I'd really just been to the WAVES.

I think at this point I would like to say that of course, being Director of the Marine Corps Women's Reserve was about the only really spectacular thing I've done in my life, that was over and above what many women in my position had done in the way of public service or in the way of private charitable organizations, and matters like that.

Q: And incidentally was the only paying job?

Streeter: The only paid job I ever had. Most of the other jobs, I had to contribute to, instead of having them contribute to me.

So of course, it became a very, very important part of my life, mostly because of the fact that our three sons were already in the armed forces, and this is something which

I might perhaps comment on at this point. Of the four directors, two others were single women. Colonel Oveta Culp Hobby had children but they were all under the age of ten. I was the only one of the four who had sons in the service. All our sons were in the service, and they were all in the sorts of jobs that were expendable.

This does not mean that I was either more or less fitted to be a director than the others were. The others were excellent and most efficient at their jobs. It merely meant that perhaps I was under a little more emotional strain. All my eggs were now in one basket. And I was very glad that they were, have always been grateful to the Marine Corps for giving me a chance to have a part in what was going on in World War II. I just mention this because it was perhaps somewhat unusual.

Q: Would you deal with another phase of this which interests me very much, and that is the fact that, when you asked your husband what he thought of this assignment that was being offered to you, he said, "If it is offered, I think you should do it."

This brings up a question. As you relate the events in your life with him, it seems to me that both he and you were very anxious that the other partner to the marriage should achieve what he wanted or she wanted to achieve, that there was the utmost cooperation in this sort of thing; would you comment on that?

Streeter: I think that's very true. It is of course one of the nicest things about our marriage. I sometimes think that mothers' stake in sons in the armed forces is over-emphasized. Fathers feel just as badly as the mothers do when anything happens to their sons. But nobody seems to sympathize with the fathers. They're supposed to be brave men and keep a stiff upper lip and all that. They're just as worried and concerned about it as the mothers are. And so Tom of course was just as worried about our three boys as I was. And very anxious if one of us could do something, he was very glad to cooperate.

As it happened, it worked out very well, because he was really over age and our daughter was only 16 so she was under age, so they took care of each other during the three years that I was away, and they got to know each other very well and have a very nice relationship.

Q: But even beyond that particular incident, he seemed always to be most tolerant of your doing other things, and approving of your doing other things outside of the home. You in turn approved of him when he wanted to retire at a relatively early age; you said, "If that's what you want to do, yes."

Streeter: Yes. Well, don't you think that's the way it ought to be?

Q: It doesn't always work that way.

Streeter: I suppose not. But although each of us was interested in different things, we still liked to talk to the other one about the things we were interested in, and the other one was interested in return. I think he found that my life was considerably more interesting to discuss at the dinner table than if it was nothing except how bad the children were this morning, what trouble I had with the cook this evening, all the rest of it. I never did learn to play bridge. So I think perhaps we had unusually interesting joint lives as well as our separate lives.

Q: Well, now, go back to the first news of the pending appointment.

Streeter: Apparently it was all sewed up before we knew much about it, unless I fell flat on my face when I went in for the interview.

Q: How did this happen, that it should be all set up?

Streeter: Well, that's all set forth in the little blue pamphlet which the Marine Corps has made available, and at this point, I think I'd better mention that because this was such an important part of my life for three years, I do want to be a little careful as to what I say about it, to be sure that it reflects what my real attitude was toward the Marine

Corps and what the attitude of the Marine Corps was to the women. And both of these things are set forth in publications. I've mentioned the publication from the Marine Corps which is obtainable from the history section of the Marine Corps, and it is their view of what the women achieved and how they functioned. Then, I must admit that I later on wrote and published a little book called Tales Of An Ancient Marine which was written primarily for my grandchildren, most of whom have not I think read it yet, but maybe they will some day.

Anyhow, it reflected my feeling about the Marine Corps, and I think that I expressed quite fully my admiration for them, my affection really for them, and how generous I think they were to me, and how devoted I was to what I was trying to do there for them.

So, in case what I may say today is perhaps sort of hodge podge, if you really want to know the true story, look back at those two books, and you'll have a very good picture of the situation.

Q: We'll keep that in mind, but I think you still should relate some of the things today.

Streeter: Well, what in particular would you like to know, Mr. Mason?

Q: Recount the story of Basil O'Connor relating this news to your husband.

Streeter: Well, a very old friend of ours who had first worked in my husband's law office in Boston was Basil O'Connor. And when Tom moved over to New York, at the time we were married, he suggested to Doc O'Connor that he come over and Tom would give him some of his business and see how he made out in New York.

So he seemed to be doing all right for a few years, and one fine day we woke up and found that he was the law partner of the Governor of New York. The firm was then called Roosevelt and O'Connor. And as Mr. Roosevelt went on and became President, he and Doc I think were still very good friends, and kept in close touch with each other. Doc, I think was his executor after his death, and certainly was his attorney. And of course, he was an old friend of ours, so we saw him quite often.

Tom was in New York, on a certain Thursday as I remember it in January, and Doc asked to see him, and told him all about this formation of the Women's Reserve, and the fact that they would like to suggest to me that I become Director.

This was a complete surprise both to Tom and to me, when he came back to tell me about it, and I'd been asked to go in the next day to be interviewed by Colonel Waller and Major Rhoades.

Q: Waller was then head of the Reserves.

Streeter: He was head of the Division of Reserves and he had been delegated by the Commandant, General Holcomb, to put into effect the plans which the Marine Corps had already by this time pretty well formulated. Major Rhoades was a friend and actually Colonel Waller's attorney in civil life. He'd been an officer in World War I in the Army, so apparently, as nearly as I can make out, General Holcomb said, "If I've got to have the women, I've got to have somebody in charge in whom I've got complete confidence." So he called on General Waller. General Waller said, "If I've got to be responsible for the women, I've got to have somebody in whom I have complete confidence," and he called on Major Rhoades.

So then the two of them came out to interview me. And the way it finally worked out was that, since there was not time for me to go to officers training school, and I was to be commissioned and put to work within a month, then, for about six months, Major Rhoades was my - what do they call it in the Navy? "Running Mate"? something like that. Anyhow we had desks side by side.

Q: This was your request, was it not?

Streeter: No, indeed.

Q: It was not?

Streeter: No. But I was delighted to have it so. This was the way they had arranged it. Most thoughtfully, because I would not have had the slightest idea how to get things done in the Marine Corps. It's not at all the way it's done in civilian life. And they knew that. They didn't have time to send me to officers training school and so they gave me somebody to sit beside me and tell me, "Now, if you want to get this done, this is the way to do it. Or, maybe this suggestion isn't the sort of thing we can do in the Marine Corps at all."

So this is the way I was trained for about six months, and I was always very grateful for it, and always had a very warm feeling of friendship for Major Rhoades for being so patient with me, because I'm sure I must have tried his patience a good deal.

Q: At the end of six months, you terminated this period.

Streeter: Well, at the end of six months, it dawned upon me that not Colonel Hobby, and not Captain (Mildred) McAfee and not Captain (Dorothy) Stratton had running mates - and I didn't think this was a very dignified position to put me in. When I went to call on them, they had their own offices, with one desk in them, which was their desk. Although I realized that in that length of time I couldn't have learned all there was to know about how to do things in the Marine Corps, at least I had some advice and training.

So I put up a memo to General Waller, and it was not approved all along the line, but it finally reached him, and he took it under consideration.

Well, about that time we had asked the heads of the other women's services, the other three directors, to come down to Camp LeJeune, so that we could show them our training that the women Marines were going through down there. So they all came, and Captain McAfee and I among others, we had quite a long talk about things. And she told me at that time I should be very grateful for having had somebody advise me until I found my way around. She had not had that, and she'd come in completely unprepared for the methods used in the military services, and she felt that she'd been unfortunate in making certain mistakes in the beginning, entirely innocently, which had however stirred up a certain feeling against her in the Navy, and that I was very lucky to have had this teaching as I went along - which I certainly have always appreciated. But I felt that, you know, you can't stay in leading reins forever.

Q: Was this in effect what you said to Colonel Waller?

Streeter: I think it was. I think I said the Marine Corps wasn't getting its money out of me.

Q: And that you were ready to take over.

Streeter: That I thought it would be more dignified for them and for me if they felt I could do so, for me to take over.

So Colonel Waller approved it, especially after I repeated to him, this remark of Captain McAfee's, because he said, "Now you realize just what we were doing. We were trying to keep you from making those mistakes."

So I thought that was really very wise of them.

Q: They were being super-cautious too, weren't they.

Streeter: No, no, I would have fallen flat on my face, I'm sure, if they hadn't somehow done something like that for me.

Q: When your husband talked to Basil O'Connor, did O'Connor reveal what kind of characteristics or talents they were seeking in a director?

Streeter: No. The interesting thing about that was that, two divergent lines met. General Holcomb called on Colonel Waller, he was then. Colonel Waller called on Major Rhoades. Major Rhoades had been a classmate of Basil O'Connor at Harvard Law School. He knew that O'Connor was close to the President, and he knew that he was pretty well posted on things that were going on, both in Washington and in the civil world. And he wrote O'Connor and said to him, "Now, this is our situation, have you any suggestions to make?"

At that point, O'Connor knew us, knew what I had been feeling and what I was frustrated about and was looking very much for something that would be really helpful to do, although heaven knows I never aspired to be director of anything. So I think he was the one who made the suggestion.

As you know, it was passed along the line probably to Dean Gildersleeve and I knew one or two people on that advisory committee too, and so, I think they had looked me up very well before they ever asked me anything. But I didn't know anything about it until the night before I went in to be interviewed.

Q: Now, to make the story complete, you must tell about the swearing in ceremony and Colonel Knox.

Streeter: Well, this is a little repetitious of some of the things I've said in Tales Of An Ancient Marine, but it's too good to be left out, because, when I went down to be interviewed by General Holcomb, Colonel Waller took me up and we met and I was asked a great many questions, but the question that I was asked repeatedly was, whether I knew any Marines?

And as a matter of fact, I didn't know any Marines. No particular reason why I should have known any Marines, because I had no military connections with any of the services, as it happened. It was a long time since there had been a war, and our paths just didn't cross.

But as I kept being asked again and again, did I know any Marines? I began to feel this is worse and worse, I've lost my chance, I don't know the right people. But I still had to be truthful about it.

It turned out later that this was an advantage, because they were afraid, if I had known other Marines, that I would not be easily disciplined to go through channels. I would have been inclined to go to any friends I might have had to help me out.

After the interview, I came down to Colonel Waller's office and he said, "Well, I think that went pretty well. But of course an appointment like this will have to have the approval of the Secretary of the Navy."

I said in a wee small voice, "Well, I don't think you'll have any difficulty there, because Secretary Knox comes from New Hampshire. He knows my mother very well. He knows my father-in-law and my mother-in-law very well, and my husband used to be his personal counsel."

So they didn't have any trouble with Secretary Knox.

Q: What was the response to that?

Streeter: Well, he looked slightly aghast. But at least it

smoothed the way. And Secretary Knox was kind enough to swear me in himself, when I was commissioned.

Q: Tell me about the official record saying that Dean Gildersleeve's committee had the role in the suggestion of a head for the Marine Corps.

Streeter: Well, as set forth in this booklet published by the Marine Corps, they evidently did, and I always understood that they did, submit several names. Then I think the Marine Corps itself proceeded to look them up and see which ones they thought would work out. And I have heard it said that the Marine Corps was open minded as to whether or not to take a professional woman, who already held a high job in some profession or of some sort. And of course, if you do that, you're bound to get someobdy who has certain qualities that you're going to want in a leader. But it is also true, and this was apparently the approach that the Marine Corps used, that no profession at that time directly fitted a woman to operate in a military organization, which does things very very differently from what an ordinary profession or business will do for them. And so, when they found that I complied with the qualifications as set forth legally, but had had a wide background, and was not specifically involved in one sort of thing which would require a complete turnover to function under a different system, apparently this seemed to them an advantage. I guess the proof of the pudding was in the eating. It did work in the end.

Q: You might add that little note about the insistent questioning on the part of General Holcomb, "Did you know anybody in the Marines?" What was back of that question?

Streeter: Well, what was the back of it was, that they were afraid that instead of going through channels, whenever I wanted to accomplish something, I would skip a few channels and go to anybody with whom I might have a personal friendship or acquaintance. I might jump over several colonels' heads to go to a general, or I might jump over the commandant's head to go to Secretary Knox, but that's something I never did do. Never would have occurred to me to do it.

Q: They were concerned about preserving the chain of command.

Streeter: They were concerned about discipline. And very rightly so, I think. It would have been a very difficult situation.

Q: As far as I know, it didn't happen in any of the services, did it?

Streeter: Well, I think we were indoctrinated early. That's what you don't do.

Q: Well, you were selected, and you were installed as Director on the 13th of February, 1943.

Streeter: Yes, that's right. And that was interesting. I think I told in my book something about that, and about the good cooperation I had from the press, always. I think I had almost better cooperation than anybody in any of the services, certainly better than the WAC had. Which I think was largely due to the prestige of the Marines, of course, and the fact that they're a very colorful outfit, and were doing a perticularly good job in the Pacific.

Q: Don't you think your personality had something to do with it also?

Streeter: Well, I don't know. But I always tried to be fair with the press, and they were fair with me. Every once in a while they'd ask me a question and I'd say, "Look, you know I can't answer that, so why do you ask me?" And they wouldn't be mad.

Q: Had you had experience with the press prior to this ever?

Streeter: No - oh, some. A little bit. But the one thing they won't stand for is somebody trying to pull the wool over their eyes, and I never tried to do that.

Q: Were you witty in dealing with them?

Streeter: Oh, some. Well, I mean, I liked them in general and we got along very well together.

Q: Could you brief them off the record and they honored this?

Streeter: As I remember it, I seldom did that. It's better not to, if you can avoid it. Usually they ask you pretty fair questions and you can give them a fair answer. I think it's better not to go off the record unless it's rather important.

Q: You might make a statement at this point as to the intention of the Marine Corps in setting up this Women's Division. What did they envision?

Streeter: Yes, I'd be glad to do that, because it interests me enormously, of course, what's going on in the armed forces at the present time, the Marines and the others too, whereby they have apparently entirely abolished any such thing as even the rather ephemeral Marine Corps Women's Reserve. At the time, in World War II, having women in uniform was a new idea. It wasn't a completely new idea, because the English especially and the Canadians had already had this system at work, and they were seen around the streets of Washington, all these other service women, and it was known to be valuable. Still it was rather difficult for a lot of people to take, and we sometimes got kind of mean remarks or nasty remarks made about the women, which were difficult for us to take.

I think that it was very essential at that time for parents especially to think that there was some woman in each of the services who would keep an eye on the women's interests, and the women's interests as distinguished from the men's interests.

Now, they're supposed to be indistinguishable. I'm not entirely sure that I agree with that point of view. Whether it is possible to operate under that system now or not, I don't know, but I'm sure it would not have been possible in 1942, because none of the armed forces can operate without the public opinion behind them. We've got to have the support of public opinion, and public opinion had gone along with them as far as having women in uniform was concerned, but they still wanted to feel that if the girls had troubles they could go to somebody who would understand. And it was our job to interpret the military to the women. It was our job equally to interpret the women to the military. We were a bridge of understanding between the two.

Then also of course we had women's officers with the enlisted women, and one of the things that in the Marine Corps we were very particular about was that the women officers should be easily accessible to the enlisted women. If they had troubles they could come and talk about it with their women officers. Generally through the sergeant.

Q: To be quite specific, it was recognized that the directors of these women's groups in the various services must be women of the highest caliber, must be recognized as such. This gave status to the whole organization. Isn't that true?

Streeter: Yes, I think so.

Q: Was that not one of the criteria for the women's committee that was supposed to be concerned about selection?

Streeter: I would assume so. And of course, although I had not had any professional job, any paid job, I had had a finger in a good many different pies here in New Jersey, and served on the State Relief Council in the worst part of the Depression, been nine years on the County Welfare Board, and a number of such things. I'd worked with both men and women, which I've always found easy to do, with both of them. And this is unusual. Ordinarily you work better with the men or you work better with the women, but not necessarily with both of them, and I was fortunate in liking both and apparently being able to talk with both of them on the same wavelength.

Q: Yes. On this level, in that day, there was real concern in the country at the possibility of the admixture of men and women in the military service - the dangers to women as a result of this - was there not?

Streeter: Oh, there always is, when you put men and women together.

Q: But less so today, don't you think, with the freedom and the relaxed way they look at things?

Streeter: Probably more damage goes on today, but nobody regards it as damage.

Q: Yes, the world's standards are so different from what they were in 1940.

Streeter: You can't compare the two. I gather that the women's services have broadened their concepts the same as the civilian people have.

Q: But in that day they had not.

Streeter: Oh, no.

Q: And therefore that responsibility fell on the shoulders of the director.

Streeter: Well, they held the buck, as it were, but it fell on the shoulders of each one, all the way down the line.

And they really felt that way about it. I remember one day, some woman in the streets of Washington - people used to stop me and talk to me, perfect strangers - and she was complimenting the Women Marines. She said, "You know, they have a certain dignity."

I said, "Well, now that you mention it, I think they do. It wouldn't have occurred to me but I think that's true."

You know, they had a certain reserve. They always looked well. They held themselves well. They had a certain dignity. And that was each one of them, not just the officers or not certain officers.

Q: Did you not have this concern reflected to you when you went on recruiting trips?

Streeter: Oh, yes.

Q: Can you recall any of those?

Streeter: Well, I just talked, mostly, to the parents. You know, about it.

Q: But they wanted to be sure their daughters would be safe.

Streeter: Yes. They wanted to think that somebody was keeping an eye out for them. And of course, I couldn't keep two eyes on 20,000 people, but all the way down the line, there was the feeling that, you look out for your people. Of course, this is the officers of any service, I think, that are properly trained, to try to look after their men or their women as the case may be, and very strongly so in the Marine Corps. One of their special traditions.

And so it's all done by handing down responsibility to the people on the different levels.

Q: But you yourself at the top have to reflect this sense of responsibility and reliability.

Streeter: Sure. Well, why wouldn't I? That's the way I felt about it.

Q: And this was perhaps one reason for your selection.

Streeter: Well, of course, I don't know. Now I think maybe I'll tell you a story. There were times when I had to be severe, and I was. I mean, you're not going to have discipline unless you react, against certain things, as well as in favor of certain things. You try to avoid having disciplinary problems by avoiding the things that cause them, the circumstances that cause them, but you're going to have them.

Human nature being what it is, there are going to be some people that are always going to be in difficulties of one sort of another.

You are tolerant and understanding, up to a point, but there can be a point at which you've got to put the foot down. And there were a few times when things got up to me, and I had to put my foot down. Otherwise, if I had excused X, I would have had to excuse A, B, C, and D all the way down the line too, and you can't do that.

Many years after the war was over, I think about 20 years after, I got a letter from a sergeant, former sergeant in the Women Marines, who was apparently a very capable office worker, and had gotten quite an important job in the Veterans Administration, and she had been a Women Marine in World War II.

She wrote me out of the blue sky, and she said, "I've never seen you. I've never heard you speak. But I do want to tell you that I think the organization of the Women Marines was so much better than anything that I've found since."

So I wrote her back and thanked her for this. It was a nice letter. And I thought particularly, how she ever missed seeing me or hearing me speak, I don't know, because I went to all the big outfits, and I usually managed to have them get together so I could speak to them. But she had been in a small detachment, and I didn't get to all the ten or dozen small detachments around about, which worked rather on their own, recruiting, some of them were, or whatever it might happen to be.

So I wrote her back, and I was pleased about it, and she wrote me back in another letter, and she ended up saying, "P.S., I felt that you loved us all."

Q: That's the personal element that got injected into it.

Streeter: Yes. This after I'd spanked some of them really pretty hard.

Q: Well, isn't that sometimes evidence of love? Concern?

Streeter: Well, it is, but they don't always think so. And I thought, this from somebody who had never seen or heard me was something.

Well, you know, I never would have dared show that to the Marine Corps. They would have thought that was sappy.

But, you cant' treat - well, I don't think you can treat women exactly the way you treat men. You know. You've got to mother them a little bit. It doesn't hurt the men any either.

Q: Tell me about your immediate problems when you took office?

Streeter: Oh, I had so many of them, I haven't any idea. They were all problems.

Q: Perhaps you can relate some of them. You had to get the organization under way.

Streeter: Well, you see, this is where Major Rhoades helped me very much and where all the advanced planning helped me. I didn't have to start any of it. I stepped into it. And this is very clearly set forth in that booklet. They didn't make any announcement of the fact that they were going to take women until they had gotten the whole framework set up at Headquarters Marine Corps. Then all they did was push the button. Then the wheels turned. And one of the things that was most helpful was that the WAVES arranged to take our enlisted training and our officer training for the first three months in with the WAVES, and this was a tremendous help to us, because at the end of that time, we set up our own training cadres down at Camp LeJeune, but we had to have someobdy to be in charge of them, and it would have taken us three months or so, somehow or other, to train enough people to run them. The officers were trained at Mt. Holyoke and the enlisted were trained at Hunter College, along with the WAVES. They had men Marines, officers in charge, and men drill instructors, and then finally, when we were moved down to Camp Lejeune, we had our own officers.

Q: Did you make trips to Holyoke and Hunter?

Streeter: Oh, yes. Oh, yes. I was down to the commissioning of the officers every second month. They had about two months indoctrination. So I guess I was at a commissioning almost every class. Either they were the junior class or the senior class.

Q: One of the things that Colonel Waller says you contributed was the contribution of ideas. You were always throwing out ideas. I wish you'd comment on that.

Streeter: He was a little frank about that.

Q: He said 50 percent of them were rejected.

Streeter: Yes, he said 50 percent of them were no good. It was easier for him to sit there and throw out the 50 percent screwy ones, instead of wondering what was happening in the Women's Marine Corps anyhow.

Q: Tell me about some of the ideas that were accepted and considered good?

Streeter: I can't remember. I do remember that at the end of our first year, I wrote an annual report and sent it up to General Waller, as he was then. And he went off to Hawaii on a tour of inspection, and he left it to his executive officer, who was an old line Marine, to deal with. And he was very good for me, because he really was an old line Marine, and I knew if I got anything past him, nobody else in the Marine Corps would object. And he was a very square shooter. If he had any objections he always made them and discussed them with me. And if he passed them, I knew they were all right.

Well, he looked at this thing. He said, "Colonel Streeter, the Marine Corps doesn't issue annual reports. It's 170 years old, and it doesn't issue annual reports."

I said, "Well, you know, we're only a year old, and I just thought you might be interested."

I withdrew my recommendations. I said, "If this isn't the proper form to put them in, I'll put them in another form some time."

That was, I suppose, typical of the different approaches. Every board of trustees I'd served on had an annual report. At the end of every year you said whether it had been successful, whether it had not, and if not, why not, and how could you do better the next year, and so on and so forth. So I just thought after we'd been there a year, maybe the Marine Corps would like to know how I thought they were doing.

Well, this was a brand new idea to the Marine Corps — they really didn't know what to make of it.

Q: Were there other annual reports?

Streeter: No. That was the only one I ever submitted. It got chopped up, and you know, if there was something that really should be taken up and acted on, it was, and the rest was discarded, for the time being, anyhow.

Colonel Gale, his name was, and he was very good for me. He used to jolly me once in a while. Good for me too.

Q: Tell me about your realization, again through the good offices of Colonel Waller, that you were director but you didn't have anything to direct.

Streeter: He told me so, in so many words.

Q: This must have come as a shock to you.

Streeter: Oh, it did. I nearly turned in my suit and everything else.

Well, I made the mistake of going to Colonel Waller for sympathy over something or other, I've forgotten what. I said, "You know, Colonel, it's a little hard on me. I've got so much responsibility and no authority."

He said, "Colonel Streeter, you have no responsiblity either." That's right, I never did have.

Q: You mean no responsibility?

Streeter: No responsibility and no authority - well, that was sort of a blow to me. And I think it was perhaps fortunate for me that nobody else besides Colonel Waller realized that I had no authority. They never were quite sure how much authority I did have, and this was quite a help.

Q: How did this stack up with the director of the WAVES and the others?

Streeter: Oh, they didn't have any either. I don't know about Colonel Hobby. But this was one of Captain McAfee's problems. I guess probably Captain Stratton's too. See, we were staff officers. We weren't line officers. We had all been used to - if we were the responsible head of an organization, we had authority - and it was a great surprise, I think, to all of us. We weren't used to being staff officers. We were used to being executives. And we had to adapt ourselves. And it wasn't so bad after all. It took a little getting used to. But as Colonel Waller told me, he said, "Now, look. You are never, in an organization like this, going to get to first base without the understanding and cooperation of a dozen other people at least. And so," - you know, things were always coming over my desk with a letter along the side and every officer who saw it initialed it, and if I wanted anything done, I had to clear it with not only my own people, up this line, but with all the people on the side that might be interested too. And it worked. I had no difficulty with it after I once understood the reason for it.

Q: But you certainly couldn't be a lone wolf.

Streeter: Oh, no. Well, I think they were quite right. You can't be a lone wolf in a military organization. And then, they've got this business of replacements. As I said, when I asked him if he'd mind if I broke my neck flying, "Oh no, the Marine Corps is set up to deal with people who break their necks." They've always got a replacement.

And when Colonel Towle came on as assistant director, he said, "Now, you've got to tell her everything you do, why you do it, how you do it, what your reason for doing it is, so that if anything happens to you, she'll know how to carry on. After she's carried on for a bit she'll have her own ideas, but at least there'll be no gap if anything happens to you."

Very sensible.

Q: When you reflect on it, did the system in any way limit your own spontaneity, your approach to things? You do have ideas that just bubble out, and was there any restriction on them because of the system?

Streeter: Oh, no. They just batted me down.

Q: But this in time becomes discouraging.

Streeter: Well, I figured that was part of the game. I mean, if I put up an idea, maybe it was haywire. Maybe they knew it wouldn't work. And anyhow, all I was entitled to do was put it up and make the best argument I could for it. Yes, I got batted down quite a lot. Everybody gets batted down in the military service. There's no use - I'm not pretending this was a bed of roses. You get thwarted, frustrated. One of the things I believe they have - I don't know if they're on fitness reports for the military or not but they are in business, "How does he or she deal with frustration?" Well, you'd jolly well better learn. In the military, you're frustrated all the time.

But, you learn to deal with it. Don't you think so?

Q: Well, I guess you do.

Streeter: You have to. No use being sour about it.

I thought I had some bright ideas, very bright ideas that were knocked out. But nevertheless, you go along all right.

Q: How did you present your bright ideas?

Streeter: Oh, I sent them up the line.

Q: In memo forms?

Streeter: Yes. To my immediate superior in command.

Q: And they were entirely spontaneous.

Streeter: Yes. He either approved them or disapproved them or put them in the wastebasket.

I suppose I might perhaps at this point say that this system worked during World War II, because of the tremendous motivation that everybody had in the middle of war, you know. We were scared. At the time I went in, we were licked. Imagine, sinking ships right off Atlantic City. And out in California, they were burning smudge pots in their back yards, as if that would ward off the Japanese planes if they ever got that close.

There was a tremendous actual fear that we would be attacked, and a knowledge that we had a long, long way to fight back before we were ever going to get the edge, if we did. And people just gave it all they had, which is something that anybody who hasn't lived through as severe a war as that probably has no conception of.

Of course, as time went on, I realized that this was a very cumbersome way, and really that the position of

Director of Women's Reserve, if it was going to exist at all, should have more status. But I wasn't going to fight about it in the middle of a war. I was doing pretty well. If I needed backing up, I generally was able to get it, and if not, it probably was because it wasn't a very good idea in the first place.

But Colonel Towle and I used to discuss this, and after the Reserves were demobilized at the end of World War II, she went back to the University of California, where she had been before she was commissioned, and was assistant dean of women there for a couple of years, until General Cates brought her back as Director of Women after the women became regulars. At that time, she had quite a talk with him, and told him that she thought the position should be more accurately described and set up than it had been in World War II, and of course they were regulars at that time, that made some difference.

So in the end, she had the standing of the Director of Reserve or the Director of Plans and Policies or the Quartermaster, or Paymaster, she was on the staff of the Commandant. And when the Commandant had weekly meetings, she was at them.

Of course I never got within arm's reach of the Commandant unless he sent for me for something or other. Eventually I reported directly to the Director of the Division of Reserve through his Exec, of course, and then the Division of Reserve head reported to the Commandant, but I never was on the Commandant's staff at all and so, after the women became regulars, the woman who was "Director of Women," not the "Women's Reserve" but of "Women," at that time, was on the Commandant's staff. And this was true until last fall, when they were finally and completely integrated, and any possible shadow of difference, for women, was abolished.

We have a woman Brigadier General now, but that's because she's Director of Information. She's in a Brigadier General's slot as Director of Information. She has nothing to do with the women. Nobody has anything to do with the women, as such.

And I think that probably, at the present time, that's okay. I'm sure it wouldn't have been in the beginning, but that's 35 years ago. And now, I think it's a different story.

Well, is there anything particular more I can say - would you like me to think about it a little time?

Q: Yes. I note a quotation from your writings, in which you talk about the fact that you tried during your tour of duty there to conduct your office with dignity, military efficiency, and humanity, and perhaps you'd give me an interpretation of that. You intimated off tape that it had to do with being available and giving counsel and so on.

Streeter: Well, of course, in a rigid structure such as a military organization, there are very definitely certain things you can't do, no matter whether you think they'd be a good idea or not. But if you look around, you can sometimes find situations that can be ameliorated. For instance, we had eventually, when they built barracks especially for women, we had certain parts of the building that the men's barracks didn't have. For one thing, we had a laundry. We did our own laundry, so - you know, we always looked fresh and cool. We weren't fresh and cool but we looked so because we washed our uniforms every night ourselves.

We also had two sort of, I don't know what you'd call them. They were quite large reception rooms, one downstairs and one on the second floor, and the reception room downstairs was for the women and their dates. The men could come and visit with them there. The one upstairs was just for the women, and they could lounge around there, if they had any spare time, you could lounge - they could lounge around there in their dressing gowns and relax. And little things like that were a great help, and we tried to think of them. They didn't cost much and they were just a little consideration.

Q: There was some concern for their privacy, was there not?

Streeter: Oh, yes.

Q: And cubicles.

Streeter: Yes, there was. Well, now, for instance, one thing that they used to do in those reception rooms, and the officers would quite often do this. The officers, some of them were very musical. Classical music. They would have records and record players and they would give a concert every once in a while for the enlisted women, most of whom had never heard any classical music in their lives. And were very much taken by it, enjoyed it.

And things like that. The officers themselves thought of doing it. That was no suggestion of mine.

Another thing that the officers did, the women officers, in two or three of the larger camps where they had specially constructed bachelor officer quarters, they had a big dining room and they had a big kitchen. Now, they had to have, what is it they call it? A TO, Table of Organization, to have cooks and bakers and KP and people to wait on table and all that. If the officers used one of those T.Os to man their kitchen and dining room, they're taking it away from some of the enlisted, who otherwise might have two sets of cooks and KP and all that.

All but one of the camps, the officers voted not to do so. They ate in a corner of the general mess. They had no special service. If they wanted to have a beefsteak party for their boy friends, they got the beefsteaks and cooked them themselves.

Now, this was something in which there was no command from above. Each station was allowed to do this of its own accord, if it wanted to. And I'm sure that it was a great morale builder. The girls did not come in with the general idea of waiting on other women. They came in to, you know, win the war. I think it was a great morale builder that we didn't ask them to.

Q: This is much later in the WAVES, but Captain Quigley told me that during her tour of duty (it's no longer called WAVE :) but during her tour of duty as head of the organization, she traveled a great deal, and she particularly concentrated on the enlisted women, thinking the officers were much more capable of looking after their own affairs.

Streeter: Well, that's so. But I concentrated on the officers to see that they were looking after the enlisted women. Which is what they're supposed to do.

Q: So you delegated the authority.

Streeter: Well, I wanted to know, for them to tell me. You don't do it in the Marine Corps anyhow - jump over your officers' heads to go talk to the enlisted women.

Q: I see.

Streeter: Hardly ever. There's one picture of me talking to the sergeants, down at the big air station in Carolina. The senior woman officer asked them if they would like to talk to me. They said they would, so she called a meeting and we sat around and talked.

I always, I made a point, in going to the camps, not to stay with the commanding officer and his wife if I could avoid it. They sometimes asked me, and I explained that I appreciated it very much, their hospitality, but as I so seldom got to see the Women Marines, I thought it was very productive if I went and stayed in the officers quarters with them, with the women officers. So I always used to. I got to spend the nights with them. You know, put on our dressing gowns, let our hair down, sit around on the floor and talk, which is the way you get to know them.

Q: Just as a matter of footnote, was the invitation that came forth from the commanding officer and his wife, for you to stay with them, was this in a sense a consideration of the fact that you were a woman?

Streeter: No, that I was a visitor, I think. No, I don't think so. It's just that I was a visitor. You know I didn't have high rank as compared with a lot of the men, but I was the ranking woman officer.

Most of them were very, very nice to me. And I was

a little bit sticking out my neck to suggest that I would rather do something else, but I thought it was important, and I really learned a lot that way.

And they got to know me, and all that. At the end, when we had so many places, I would usually try to go to the larger camps once a year, and the Assistant Director, Colonel Towle, would go the six months in between. So that somebody from headquarters got down to find out what was going on.

Q: What use did you make of the chaplain's group?

Streeter: Oh, very much.

Q: Tell me about it.

Streeter: I'm a great believer in the chaplains, and in the Red Cross officers. We didn't have very many. I think we only had about two or at the most three, camps where we had Red Cross officers. But they and the Chaplains are the only two people in the camp that are not in the chain of command, and boy, I leaned on them heavily. They could talk to me frankly about what they thought about things that were going on. I don't mean that I ducked the chain of command because it really is poisonous to avoid your chain of command. You've got to go through your chain of command, except for the chaplains and the Red Cross people.

The chaplains were very good.

Q: Can you recall any specific instance where the chaplain was of special use to you?

Streeter: Not particular ones. But if I was concerned about, you know, reactions at the camp or something like that, I would generally go to them and say, "What have you got on your mind?"

Q: Did you employ them in any way in an educational sense?

Streeter: No. I didn't employ anybody in any sense.

Q: I mean, instigating a program say at LeJeune or some place for the women that had to do with morale building, one phase or another?

Streeter: No. I think that's the officer's job. No. I had to be very careful not to go outside the chain of command. I once had to relieve a company commander who persisted in going outside of her lieutenants and sergeants and having sort of her own private mouth pieces around the outfit, and the whole morale of the company was bottom level. I explained to her, it wasn't the thing to do, but she couldn't seem to get out of the habit.

Q: A carry over from private life, wasn't it?

Streeter: I suppose. I don't know. But you have to be particular about that. And what you find, and this it took me a little while to discover, but it was most helpful, after I discovered it - things come to you. I could not go out snooping. Very, very bad if I went out snooping, around the camps. If there's something going on that isn't quite right, somebody will get the word to me. I don't have to go out sniffing around. The word will come back to me and I'll check it.

See what actually *is* going on. They were just as concerned as I was with the good performance of the women.

Q: What was your policy vis-a-vis men-women relationships in camps?

Streeter: Don't ask me that with a straight face. Didn't make much difference what my policy was.

Q: Yes, I'm sure it didn't. Human nature is human nature.

Streeter: Yes. But the Marine Corps had a policy, in

common with all the others, I don't know about the Army, but the other Navy components. And if women got pregnant, which I suppose is what you're talking about, they were discharged for the convenience of the government, under a medical discharge, and that's all that was ever said about it. They were not discharged for pregnancy or anything like that. And it was not considered a black mark, except that they were not allowed back again.

Q: They didn't get dishonorable discharge, they just -

Streeter: No, no. It was an honorable discharge for the convenience of the government. This was the policy of all the naval services, and I presume the Army too.

Q: Was there any follow up on a woman like that?

Streeter: No.
How could you, once she got off the camp? There were attempts on the part of especially the Red Cross, where we had a Red Cross, before she left the camp, to see what could be done about the baby. But once they were discharged, the Marine Corps couldn't get into home follow-up. You can see, it would be endless.

Q: No, but the home service of the Red Cross did? And could?

Streeter: Yes. Sometimes, they'd try.

And that's one of the things that the newspaper people sometimes asked me about: "Well, have you had any babies in barracks?"

And I just looked them in the eye and I said, "Now, look -- if anybody in the world knows about human nature, it's newspaper people, who see all kinds of it in all kinds of places. And you know I can't answer that question so please don't ask me."

And they didn't. And they never published anything about it.

Q: But if they could get a specific, it would make a headline, and they'd like to have it.

Streeter: They weren't going to get a specific.

Interview with Mrs. Ruth Cheney Streeter
(Mrs. Thomas W. Streeter, Sr.)
At her home, Morristown, New Jersey.
July 9, 1979
By John T. Mason, Jr.

Q: It's such a great pleasure to be with you, Mrs. Streeter. We, together, Betty and I have been looking forward to this. Would you resume your talk about your period in the Marine Corps as director of the Women Marines, by adding some things today. I note that in the first month after you assumed the directorship in 1943, you made an extensive tour of the country, going to the West Coast, speaking in at least sixteen major cities and in many minor ones. Would you recall some of your experiences on that trip which was quite influential because of the results in recruiting and so forth.

Mrs. Streeter: Yes, Mr. Mason. It was indeed a very active period of time. And considering how new I was in the Marine Corps, it was quite an experience for me. I think that the surge in enlistments did not have too much to do with anything that I said. It was kind of a pent up enthusiasm,

I think. The women had already begun to serve in the other branches of the armed forces, but the Marines have always had a certain glamor, and when they heard about the Marines, they came in droves.

Q: Were you in uniform on this trip?

Streeter: Yes.

Q: In the green uniform.

Streeter: Yes, that's right. I had to be. It wouldn't have made any impression at all in civies.

Q: So you became a visual symbol really of service in the Marine Corps.

Streeter: I had a little difficulty getting into a uniform. I hadn't worn a coat and skirt for years. I wore a one piece dress most of the time. And certainly not a shirt and tie.

Q: Did you know how to tie your tie?

Streeter: Yes, I remembered how to tie my tie, because I used to ride horseback a good deal, and in a side saddle, and so

I knew about ties. But I didn't tie them that way, obviously.

Well, in any case, I had got used to the uniform a little bit. It took a little while to learn how to carry oneself in uniform, rather stiffer than one ordinarily did, and try to look as military as possible.

I started out by going to Pittsburgh, and I got the key to the city of Pittsburgh from a wonderful old lady in Pittsburgh who met me at the station and represented the city, and they treated me very well, and that broke the ice a little bit, because of course I was nervous about all this, not having done it before.

Q: Your P.I. woman went with you, did she not?

Streeter: Yes. But My Public Information woman, as you call her, was Captain Louise Stewart. She was young and very, very pretty, and I guess she was about 26, 27, something like that, so her contact was mostly with the young Marines, not older people.

Q: Yes, but you were very handsome too, judging from your pictures.

Streeter: Well, that's as may be. But I appealed to the older people, the parents, which was very important, because the real reason that they had somebody called a Director of

Women's Reserve in all the services was because the parents were not going to let their little darlings go in among all these wolves unless they thought that somebody was keeping a motherly eye on them.

This the Marine Corps realized, and in a sense, that was what we stood for. And frequently I did speak not just to parents that happened to be in a big gathering, but to groups of parents across the country, and we always got along very well.

Q: You had had a lot of experience in public speaking anyway, had you not?

Streeter: Well, yes. Not on this particular subject, but I was reaonably accustomed to making speeches.

So I had a nice time in Pittsburgh. Then I went on across the country, and I got to a huge university, I don't think it was Purdue. What's the other one in Indiana?

Q: Indiana University at Bloomington, Indiana.

Streeter: I think it must have been. Anyhow, it had a big contingent of WAVES. It had a small contingent of -- no, it hadn't any Marines, I guess, at that time, although later it did, but it had a big contingent of WAVES who were taking special training at the university, and they of course were turned out for me, and had to come and listen to me speak. And I spoke in a great big auditorium there that holds several thousand people.

Q: What was your general theme as you spoke on these occasions? Was it recruitment?

Streeter: To begin with, it was to tell them how desperate the situation was.

Q: The war situation.

Streeter: The war, yes. I mean, coming from New Jersey, I was able to tell them about our ships being sunk in plain sight of Atlantic City. In the interior of the country, this was not entirely realized the way we on the coast realized it. That was the first thing, that they were needed, that this was no show, that this was a vast necessity. And then, the theme of course was always, "Free a Man to Fight." And that we could do as women in business have long been doing. There were many places where we could do just as well in this country as the men could and in some cases better.

This was our function. As I think I told you, later on the Commandant of the Marine Corps told us that without the women being in the Marine Corps, the 6th Marine Division could not have been activated. It was about the same size, same number of officers and enlisted personnel, and there just wouldn't have been a 6th Marine Division unless we had been there. There weren't men enough to go around and cover all the organizational work as well as the actual front line work.

So this point was made, and it made the women feel that they were necessary.

I was talking of course not just to parents and grown ups but to the young women themselves. And that was what they needed to feel, because not only before they enlisted but after they enlisted they so often were doing more or less the same sort of thing that they would have done in civil life. And they had to feel that being a stenographer was important, and all these other more or less routine and not especially exciting jobs were absolutely necessary, and that somebody, in this case men, would have had to do them if we weren't doing them.

So that was the sort of talk that I made wherever I went.

As I say, I didn't have to whip up any particular enthusiasm for the Marine Corps because they all had that anyhow.

And then I went across the country, and I went to Seattle, and of course down to California, and -

Q: You traveled by train?

Streeter: I think I did travel entirely by train. At this stage of the game. And of course, when I got to the West Coast, I got to the big camps, where the Marines were getting their last training.

Q: Camp Pendleton.

Streeter: Camp Pendleton and San Diego and some of the air stations. That was where I got some education about the Marine Corps. And then of course I was better able to go on and tell the civilian groups.

Now, sometimes I only had a very small group. Some of the colleges or schools that I went to might not have been more than 15 or 20. As I think I mentioned earlier in the talk, the colleges looked with sort of a dubious eye on our getting students. The alumnae of colleges flocked to us. We had many that didn't wait to be officers and were enlisted personnel.

Q: You made that point when you talked about Bryn Mawr.

Streeter: Yes. But it was true of other colleges too. They needed to keep their women students, and they did not encourage them too much. But we didn't want them too young anyhow. Twenty was our minimum age. And so we had plenty to draw from, plenty of people, and we got along all right.

Q: You say, when you went to Pendleton and other camps where the men were, where they were preparing for embarkation, you added to your own education. In what sense?

Streeter: Well, you can read about that sort of thing, but it doesn't take the place of seeing them.

Q: The urgency of the situation.

Streeter: Yes, and the sort of training that they had to go through. Again, I told you about going up with the paratroopers, making their first jump -

Q: No, you didn't, and you must tell me that. Was that on this initial trip?

Streeter: That was in California, yes, on my initial trip.

Q: All right, tell me about that. You not only went up with parachuters but you jumped from a pole or something later on.

Streeter: Well, yes, but that's different. They asked me if I'd like to go up with these men who were going up for the first time, and I said, yes, if it wouldn't make them any more nervous, I would be glad to. So we went up, and were all prepared for it, of course, and when we got to the proper height, out the door they went with their parachutes.

Q: At what height, about 10,000 feet?

Streeter: Oh, Lord no. They don't go from that height. I don't know, about three or four thousand feet or maybe less. Of course, the higher it is, the more time they've got to get everything straightened out. But also, when it comes to jumping in battle, the more time they've got to be shot down. So later on, they tried to teach them to jump from low altitudes. But these were men making their first jump, and I'm sure they were plenty nervous. But they tried not to show it.

So I inquired afterwards if there was any special recognition for first jumps and they said, well, yes, it was customary to let them have a case of beer. So I said, "Will you please let them have a case of beer from me?"

So I was popular with that group of paratroopers.

Q: You made your own jump from a tower?

Streeter: Well, yes. That's something they had at Camp LeJeune. These men also had done that. They jumped of course with a parachute. They had a tower and jumped.

Q: How high is the tower?

Streeter: It's not so very high, but they pulled a little chute out when they jumped. You see, there was an automatic thing that pulled the little chute out so they could be sure the big chute would open. It was only a few hundred feet, I've forgotten how high.

Q: It was just to get accustomed to falling, then.

Streeter: Falling, yes.

Q: And pulling the rope.

Streeter: Yes.

Q: How did you do on that?

Streeter: I didn't. They had a bench, and for the benefit of the women, we sat on a bench, and one time when I was down at Camp LeJeune, Eugenia Le Jeune, the General's daughter, daughter of the Commandant Le Jeune after whom the camp was named, was one of our officers, and she was going through Officers Candidate School, so I thought it would be just fine if Eugenia and I came down on the bench together, so, that's what we did. They hauled us up to the top of this thing and then they dropped us. Actually on the bench, we didn't have parachutes of course. They didn't cut the line. They let us down. On the wire. But you can't tell me that some enlisted man handling the wire didn't let us down with a good big thump! I'm sure he could have let us down much more easily than he did.

However, we wouldn't give him any satisfaction about that.

Q: This fright which you must have experienced didn't prevent you from clear thinking, however.

Streeter: Well, I know boys and men fairly well and this was much too good an opportunity to miss entirely.

Q: Then you went in a tank, too, you had that experience.

Streeter: Yes, I think I went in a tank, and one time they had a mockup of a plane. Of course I went in a good many planes, but this was a mockup. They had a mockup of the belly gunner, you know, and they got me into that little bubble. They had great trouble getting me out. Have you ever tried to get into one? Well, there's not much room in one, and they put small people in that position, because they only want people who would fit in, were small, but I wasn't just that small, so it was quite an experience getting me out of it, too.

Q: You tried your hand at marksmanship, too.

Streeter: Oh, yes.

Q: How were you there?

Streeter: Well, this was at Camp LeJeune too and this was when Colonel Eaton from the Canadian Womens Army Corps came down with me. We had a rainy day. So they took us over to the marksmanship for the pilots, well, not pilots, anybody, the ground troops mostly, I guess. And they had moving pictures of planes diving on you, or flying over you, and then you had a machine gun that of course didn't shoot bullets but it shot dots of light, so that you could tell whether you hit this machine coming at you head on or whether you didn't. So we spent a lively morning, Colonel Eaton and I, popping off on these things.

Q: How accurate were you?

Streeter: Not very.

Q: You would have been bombed out.

Streeter: Well, I wouldn't give much for my chances. You have to learn to lead them, of course, but I think I led them too much or something. Anyhow, I don't think I shot many down that day.

Q: Well, resume the country wide tour.

Streeter: Oh, landing ships, I forgot about landing ships also - I climbed down nets in landing ships.

Q: For beach landings, you mean?

Streeter: Yes. Well, from a ship into a landing vessel, you know. They had a practice net at Camp LeJeune so of course I had to do that too. Of course, all of this I quite enjoyed.

Q: I'll bet you did.

Streeter: I mean, it was what was being done. Had to be done by somebody.

Q: And this, I take it, was photographed?

Streeter: I don't think it was, no. I think I jumped on any idea of those being photographed. They were just experiences, if you want to call it that.

Q: Well, this country-wide tour took you to the West Coast and took you out to the Northwest.

Streeter: Seattle especially.

Q: Where else did it take you?

Streeter: Well, there and back. It took me to New Orleans.

Q: How were you received in the South? In terms of possible enlistments for the Marine Corps?

Streeter: Well, it being the South, I was always most courteously received. The enlistments from the South were not proportionately as high as the enlistments from other parts of the country, which I think you can lay entirely to the customary point of view in the South.

Q: This is what I thought probably was the case.

Streeter: Yes, it was. They still have a statue in New Orleans however to Molly Marine, one of the women Marines in uniform, which was put up by the city, I think.

Q: In a public park?

Streeter: Yes. Molly Marine is still there. We had a considerable number. But I think not as high proportionately. They were very good, the ones that did come. And of course most of our camps were either in the South or the West. So they were familiar with women. But I did go to one quite good sized air station in the South, and the air crews there were getting their flight training and then going on out to the Pacific; and we had quite an interesting and quite troublesome but understandable situation which grew up there, because the men were there for, oh, I don't know, six months or so, and the women all had friends among them, and then, they went out. And the women were left behind. And this was rather a small field so that it was a more concentrated relationship than in some of the very large air stations, and they were awfully upset because they couldn't go too. And I had to go down and, you know, calm them down. I told them, "Well, that's not our job, to go out to the Pacific. Our job is to stay here and keep things running here." And they came around very, very well, in spite of the disappointment.

Q: That was a morale problem.

Streeter: Oh, it was very much of a morale problem. But it worked out. These kids were very reasonable, and very devoted really. I mean, if you could tell them and show them that what they were doing really was helpful to the Marine Corps, they subsided. Many of their grievances subsided very quickly. That's known as morale.

Q: The net result of that first tour, in terms of statistics, is rather striking, it seems to me, and although you attribute that to a long standing residue of respect and so forth, for the Marine Corps as such, and the glamor attached to the Marine Corps, I think that one has to conclude that perhaps the fact that you went speaking and publicized it, and in person represented what the Woman Marine would be in uniform, had a great effect. I want to quote those statistics.

In the first eight weeks of existence of the Womens Corps, there were 2,495 enlistees. Within a year, there were 800 officers and 14,000 others.

Streeter: Yes, that is so.

Q: I think that's a remarkable record.

Streeter: Yes, and as it says in the Marine Corps pamphlet there, they hadn't expected to have more than six thousand when they first opened it up, and it became 18,000 enlisted and a thousand officers. I must lay most of that success to the reputation of the Marine Corps. But I think I had perhaps a certain advantage, over the other directors, intangible, but it was known of course that I had three sons, in the military service. You see, with the other directors, two were unmarried, and Colonel Hobby's children were little. Now, this, I think, helped me with the public. They knew that I had sons at the front as many of them had sons at the front. They knew that I would keep a motherly eye on their daughters, and this helped me also with the Marine Corps, I think, intangibly. They knew that I had much at stake, as they had much at stake, and it all was part of the picture that I think helped me to get along, both in the Marine Corps and in the civilian work that I did.

Q: One little tangent on enlistment, since we're on that subject, was the development of the home town platoon, so to speak. That I think is a most interesting development. Tell me about it.

Streeter: That was a good public relations gimmick. All that it amounted to really was that the women who enlisted in a certain period, in a certain city, went down together to boot camp, and they stayed together for this six weeks that they were recruits. But immediately after that, they went to wherever they could serve.

Q: They were dispersed.

Streeter: They were dispersed, because, you see, while they were at recruit depot, their skills were found out, as well as possible, and when a request came in for a detail to go in such and such a camp, they were assigned that way, so that naturally split them up, and it probably helped them through recruit depot because they were with friends. They weren't entirely strange. Although of course they didn't all know each other necessarily because they came from the same city. And they kept so busy at recruit depot anyhow, they didn't have much time to be homesick. But I think that it was a good enlistment gadget, and generally rather helpful.

Q: Helpful in terms of morale, too, I would think.

Streeter: Yes.

Q: After boot camp and still a part of training, you did intimate that the women were exposed to viewing the kind of training the men underwent. Tell me a little about that.

Streeter: Oh, this was one of the most inspiring things, as far as the women were concerned. When we had recruit depot going at full tilt, we had three companies, and each of them spent six weeks there, every –

Q: – largely LeJeune?

Streeter: Camp LeJeune, yes. And a new company came in every two weeks, so that they rotated, but each company spent six weeks there. And during that time, they were given what was called an arms demonstration, by the men instructors that instructed the men. And this was a very lifelike thing, of course, because it began with hand to hand fighting. How do you get a guy down and knife him? Then they had rifle shooting, and they had grenades. They had bazookas. They had all of these things that the men used, and what the men were going through right there at Camp LeJeune. These were the instructors that were teaching the men how to do it, put on a demonstration, so the women could see what the men's training consisted of. And it always ended up by a tank coming up a sand cliff onto the parade ground. The women sat in bleachers and watched this, you see. So every woman that went through boot camp saw one of these demonstrations.

And after things had gotten pretty well organized down at Camp LeJeune, we invited the other women directors to come down to one of these Saturday reviews. We flew them down, and they saw them, and they were all very much impressed and wished that they had something like that too, because it was so realistic.

Q: Did they get anything of that order?

Streeter: They have - they may have had something of the sort, but it wasn't realistic, I think.

Q: How did your women react to this, viewing it for the first time? In such a vivid fashion?

Streeter: Well, they were impressed. I don't know what else they were. They didn't tell me. But I was impressed myself.

The hand to hand fighting was almost the worst to watch, because that was very realistic, and all the other things were equally so. The point, I think, was, not that our men were being trained to do these things, but the Japanese were also trained to do exactly this sort of thing, and that our men had to face up to what the Japs were doing along exactly these same lines.

Q: The point was that they were the aggressors in this technique.

Streeter: Well, they were the people they had to go up against and so they had to know how to do it too.

Q: Your women went on to specialized schools also as time went on, didn't they?

Streeter: Yes. To begin with, of course, a good many of the jobs that were easiest to fill were clerical jobs. Many of these women already had clerical skills, and they were the most like civilian life that there were available, and the biggest demand for them, because they were generally much better than the men who were doing clerical work, except when it was special kinds of forms and things like that that were particular to the Marine Corps.

So, to begin with, a good many went to that kind of job. But as other jobs opened up, and as we found that they could do, for instance, driving trucks and things of that sort, then they were sent to quartermaster schools and they were sent to communications schools, and schools of that kind. They also had non-commissioned officers schools.

This all grew naturally as the supply and the demand grew, in order to fit them together.

Q: As different kinds of outlets opened up to the women.

Streeter: Right.

Q: They began with twenty different categories, I believe, did they not, of jobs?

Streeter: Well, I don't know that we pinned them down quite that much. We said, anything except heavy lifting and combat. They could try.

They were even in "secret and confidential files," which always entertained me, because they always claim that women can't keep a confidence, you know.

Q: Well, this called for a special investigation, did it not, of background?

Streeter: I suppose. Yes. I think that's where Eugenia LeJeune ended up, was "secret and confidential files."

Q: And eventually, the George Marshall Library down here in Lexington.

Streeter: Exactly.

Q: Later on, I believe, there was a new wrinkle, so to speak, in personnel matters, when it became possible, enlisted people became officers, being promoted through the ranks. Did you have that idea?

Streeter: No. That's an old Marine Corps idea, to promote through the ranks, and I think in general it is good, because they have shown a good spirit and a good efficiency as enlisted women. It gives them something to look forward to and to concentrate improving on.

In looking back, I think we felt that we sometimes cut ourselves off from later good material from civilian life.

Q: You mean, who would go in - ?

Streeter: – by promoting almost all officers from the ranks, which, about halfway through the training time, we did. We had begun to do it earlier, but an increasing number were promoted through the ranks, and that kept us from having older women, because most of the officers who enlisted at the time were in their twenties, so we had a lot of second lieutenants in their twenties, and there were some jobs that we would have been glad to have some older women in. And perhaps we over-did that a little. But I think the general idea is excellent. And it's an old Marine Corps tradition. A good many of their men are promoted that way too.

Q: I suppose a lot of women, in their enthusiasm to join in the war effort, regardless of their background and experience, just enlisted.

Streeter: Yes, they did. We had a very high proportion of people who'd had some college, and they just – well, this happened with the men too, of course. They just didn't want to wait.

Q: It must have pleased you personally and particularly, when so many of them began to be employed in the field of aviation.

Streeter: Well, yes and no. The field of aviation firmly had its feet on the ground. They weren't allowed to fly, as you know.

Q: I know that. Nor were you.

Streeter: Nor was I. There were about half of them employed in aviation, but they were all, of course, in ground work.

Q: This was Marine Aviation?

Streeter: Marine Aviation, yes. Oh, yes, they were Marines. They were in Marine uniform and everything. The Marine pilots sometimes trained with the Navy's, but not so much after they had got through their basic training. Their basic flight training, as I remember it, was largely with the Navy. But after that, they had special training for the sorts of things that the Marine pilots generally did.

But that was all beyond our cognizance. We had a large number of quartermaster personnel in aviation, a large number of communications, and especially at air fields. And, oh yes, we had mechanics. Airplane mechanics. And they were trained in Oklahoma, with the Navy, and the Navy had something like 40,000 men, and some WAVES I'm sure, there, and at one time I visited that field, and I visited it at the time of a Saturday morning review, and the commanding officer very kindly offered to let me take the review.

Well, have you ever tried reviewing 40,000 people?

Streeter #4 - 257

You get positively dizzy. They march and they march and they march. And that was quite an experience, I must say. I've taken small reviews but I had not ever taken one as big as that.

So the aviation personnel were very busy. They liked of course the things that had definitely to do with flying. Quartermaster was a job that in general the women didn't like particularly, although they recognized that it was very necessary.

Q: Did they take to the Link training?

Streeter: Oh yes, they had Link trainers. Yes.

Q: And what about the control towers?

Streeter: I'm trying to think. I think they had some, but they didn't have very many. That's really a pretty big job. It wasn't then as big a job as it is at a civilian airport now, because there wasn't the amount of flying, but I don't think that they had many in that. It's a long training.

Q: Apparently the Navy did, because Joy Hancock told me that they did so admirably in that job.

Streeter: They do. And they're doing it now.

Q: Women with their particular aptitudes were sometimes much better than the men. I mean, their attention to detail, their span of interest, that sort of thing.

Streeter: I don't know that they're better than the men, but I'm sure it's true that they're very good and that they're still doing it. And I can't think that we had very many, but we had some. I think. But it's a long training, now, several years. Mary's granddaughter is one.

Q: Oh, really?

Streeter: Yes. In the WAVES still, in the Navy. As an air controller. But it took her a long time.

Q: Well, as I say, this must have been particularly pleasing to you, as a flier, wasn't it?

Streeter: It wasn't pleasing. It was aggravating.
However, I took an interest in it.

Q: The horizon wasn't quite broad enough for you, was it?

Streeter: No, not enough.

Q: Did you visit many of the air fields?

Streeter: Oh, yes. Oh, yes. And I had a lovely time, at one of them, because they had a bombing practice. I mean, it was a - you know, a setup, and all they had was the nose compartment, and it was quite interesting, because you lay down, as I remember it, in this particular mockup, and the earth revolved under you, you see - you, of course, the mockup was standing still, but they photographed - the photograph passed on a moving thing, so you lay out in the nose, and then you pressed a button when you thought you were in the right place. I enjoyed it. The reason I enjoyed being there was, it had to be air conditioned because nobody could possibly have lived in it if they didn't, so that was the coolest place on the air station -- to get out in the nose of the mockup with your little pipe of cold air coming in on top of you.

Q: That was the place to go.

Streeter: That was the place to go. I discovered that early.

Q: This of course was toward the end of the war, but it has to do with personnel and recruitment and so forth. Would you talk about the assignment of the first thousand Marines to Hawaii?

Streeter: Oh, yes. Well, we had a very interesting time about that. The Women's Army Corps were the only people who had been allowed overseas, in the beginning, because they were an Auxiliary, at that time, and so nobody fussed about them too much, about regulating them. Then by the time the Navy personnel came along, Congress began to worry about having women overseas, and so they would never let them and never did let them go anywhere near combat. They were in Hawaii and in the safe parts of Alaska.

Q: How far afield did the women in the Army get?

Streeter: Oh, Africa and all through, certainly in Africa. I don't know how far else. But they were in Europe.

Q: Of course the nurses, the Navy nurses —

Streeter: I mean the WACs.

Q: The Navy nurses got over.

Streeter: Oh, sure, but I mean the equivalent, the Women Marines. They (WACs) were in Europe and we were not.

Q: That in itself may have been a slight deterrent to enlistment, was it not?

Streeter: No. No, I don't think so.

Q: Well, anyway, tell me the Hawaiian story.

Streeter: So I went to Colonel Hobby about that, and you see, this is where it was so nice that we all four got along very well with each other, and I don't know what my superiors thought about it, perhaps, except that it saved them a lot of bother, because I did not have to go through the Commandant of the Marine Corps and the Secretary of the Navy to the Secretary of War down to Colonel Hobby. I could pick up the telephone and talk to Colonel Hobby, "When can I come over and see you?"

This was certainly sensible and nobody fussed about it, but it was perhaps not exactly according to Hoyle.

In any case, I did go to her, and I said, "Look, Oveta, what did you find was the best way of selecting your people to go overseas?"

She said, "Well, according to their records, their military records. I can't say that the Northerners were better than the Southerners or the Westerners were better than the New York City people, for instance, or anything at all like that. Or necessarily their education or anything at all, just their records. A person who's had a good record in this country is likely to have a good record abroad, and a person who's had disciplinary problems in this country, or whose health wasn't good, we wouldn't send abroad. Sometimes you sent more mature ones than the newest enlistees."

As we only sent one group, those were the standards we used. I presume that if you were sending replacements all the time, you would modify your standards accordingly. You'd have to send a large group and so you wouldn't perhaps select them so carefully. But that was the chief method we used.

Q: Had you had basic aptitude tests for your - ?

Streeter: Oh, Lord yes.

Q: So you did know what their skills were.

Streeter: Yes. And if the people in Hawaii asked for them by, you know, their military number, their MO, what did they call it? Military Occupation number. We sent those.

Q: You went out there in October, 1944, didn't you, to see the lay of the ground and make some specific arrangements?

Streeter: Yes.

Q: Can you recall that trip?

Streeter: Yes, I will. That was a very interesting trip. I was met in Honolulu by General Waller, no less, who was then commanding officer of the garrison troops.

Q: Your old friend and critic.

Streeter: My old friend. So he put himself out to see that we saw everything, and made the right contacts and were comfortably taken care of.

Q: Who went with you?

Streeter: Marion Dryden, Major Dryden, who was the sort of head woman officer in the aviation section. See, the Marine fliers were largely trained and largely served with the Navy, and the offices of the Aviation Marine personnel were in the Navy building in the city of Washington, whereas the Marine Corps headquarters was across the river in Virginia.

So Major Dryden was the senior officer of the women in aviation. She came out with me because about half the women who'd been requested for Hawaii were to be at the air stations in Hawaii, EWA, to be precise, and the others were to be at the Marine Corps base.

The ones at the Marine Corps base were in luck because the Coast Guard had just moved out. They'd gone further west in the Pacific.

Streeter #4 - 264

Q: They'd gone to Guam?

Streeter: I don't mean the Coast Guard, I mean the construction –

Q: They'd gone to Guam, the SeaBees.

Streeter: Oh, further than that, I think.

Q: Okinawa?

Streeter: No, it wasn't as late as Okinawa, but they had gone way out. And they had left the barracks which they had built, and being construction guys, the SeaBees, they'd built themselves reasonably good comfortable barracks. They were big wooden barracks and rather nice and airy, and much better than the quonset huts that most of the WAVES were living in. And because they were vacant, we got them. I didn't do this. This had been done before I got there. So our detachment there was quite luxurious, as things go.

We sent out one of our very best women officers, and I'll remember her name presently. Major Marion Wing. She had a fine idea. They had left a small group of SeaBees behind just in case things didn't fit or needed to be changed and adjusted to what we had to have, and so this group of men SeaBees was there while we were settling in. And she had a fine way of treating men. No SeaBee could pay for a coke. As many cokes a day as he wanted and he couldn't ever pay for them. We got more work out of those SeaBees than you could ever imagine.

Q: Simple little wrinkle, wasn't it.

Streeter: Simple little wrinkle but she thought of that herself.

When I went out, of course, I was ahead of them, so I saw where they were going to be accommodated but they were not actually out there at the time.

Q: It was to be a thousand, was it not, the first contingent?

Streeter: Yes. I'm not sure it wasn't 2000 in all, about 1000 for the air station and 1000 for the base, and Major Dryden particularly was in touch with the air station, the air personnel.

I did meet Admiral Nimitz.

Q: You didn't meet him?

Streeter: I did. Oh, yes, I did. I went and called on him.

Q: Did he entertain you?

Streeter: Oh, no. He was quite formal. I just called on him in his office. He had other things to do. Well, he did. Plenty.

Q: But he was usually pretty generous in his entertaining at dinner, luncheons, that sort of thing.

Streeter: Well, I don't think he did. Various people did. But - well, I admired Admiral Nimitz of course very much, but I don't think that I ever was on familiar terms with him exactly.

So It was, I think, very helpful to have me go out there. I understood better what the situation was going to be, and I think I was able to explain it to people out there. Of course, for the first time there, I ran into Marines some of whom were back from the Pacific fighting, that had never seen any Women Marines, and so they were interested in just what they were going to be like. That's as near the front as we ever got, but that was pretty near, because when they shipped out from there, they shipped out to the front.

Q: It must have been of exceedingly great interest to all the women in the Marine Corps.

Streeter: We had no trouble getting volunteers.

Streeter #4 - 267

Q: I wouldn't think so.

Streeter: I think that one of the decisions that was made was that in the future, they would not ask for volunteers, that they would, they should arrange to be sent there the same as they'd be sent anywhere else. But at the time that they were enlisted, they weren't even allowed overseas, so we had volunteers for that.

Q: It's interesting, in reviewing the official report, to discover that every time there was a major engagement in the Pacific where Marines were heavily involved, it meant that back home more and more women were assigned to jobs bolstering and supporting here the effort in the -

Streeter: - well, yes, and I'm sure enlistments were up after any big strike out there. Well, it began to come closer to home, to people. One of the other things that I was supposed to do was to make contact with the Hawaiian people, not really the Hawaiians themselves but the Americans living in Hawaii, and prepare them for this influx of women. And they couldn't have been nicer. There is now a park, I believe, a public park, but in those days it was still in private hands. It was the home of some of the Hawaiian kings. It was like a great big city block of garden, and the old house, the old furniture. It was a beautiful place. Because where were the women going to go when they had a day off, in Hawaii? I mean there were 100 men to every woman, practically, and sometimes what they wanted to do was to get off by themselves quietly. I don't say that all of them wanted to, all of the time, but sometimes one does need something like that. And they had a very interesting arrangement there about dances, because there were all colors and kinds, you see, not just whites, and the rule was - of course, they started to have fights very quickly, and I think it was the chaplains that thought up this idea. If a Woman Marine went with a white man, she danced only with white men that night. And if she went with a black man, she danced only with black men that night.

Q: What an interesting idea.

Streeter: So there were no fights. You see, if one was cutting in on the other, it had begun to start fights, and this way there weren't any. That was a very clever idea.

Q: It certainly was.

Streeter: Well, they took us around and they showed us the different parts of Hawaii, the different stations on it, and of course it was very interesting indeed.

Q: The women were scattered around the various islands,

were they?

Streeter: No. No, they were not. They were at Oahu and at Honolulu and Ewa.

Q: All on the island of Oahu.

Streeter: I think so. I think that's right. But I was taken to the other islands, mostly to the air stations. I think that - you see, the Women Marines weren't out there very long.

Q: No, they certainly weren't.

Streeter: They didn't get out there till the end of '44, and the war was over in the summer of '45.

Then they did, some of them stayed, because of course there was a lot of processing to be done, paper work, when the men began to come back and be shipped through to this country to be demobilized.

Of course, I saw Pearl Harbor. They took me around to see Pearl Harbor. I had seen pictures, of course, but there was still a good deal of debris in those days, and the Arizona was there, and she just was, she had a wooden deck boarded over her and mast and the flag, and she was, and I believe still is, a commissioned ship of the United

States Navy. There are something like 1100 of her crew still in her, and they have put up what seems to me a perfectly dreadful memorial on top of her. It's sway backed, sort of a big oblong swaybacked flat square building. Whoever designed that and whoever approved the design, I can't imagine, but that's what they've done. And she was a lot more impressive with just her wooden deck and her mast and her flag.

Of course, that's one thing I didn't like. After the war they sent a squadron of Japanese Navy vessels to Pearl Harbor. It would have been better if they'd kept them out of Pearl Harbor. Of course they had to be saluted coming in to Pearl Harbor, a nation, fires a salute. I think it would have been better if they had omitted Pearl Harbor.

You know, it's like a great hand. You come in through a narrow channel, and then there are all the piers and all where the bay spreads out. And I think I'm right in this, the only two places where the Navy mans the rails are when they pass Mount Vernon and coming into Pearl Harbor. Every ship that comes in mans the rails.

Q: Well, Now I think this would be a fitting place for you to talk about your own philosophy, which has been termed the philosophy of hard work. Because this was something you enunciated.

Streeter: Well, I can't think that was a very novel philosophy.

Q: No, but it's something that you enunciated six months after you took over your job. I think you might talk a little about the philosophy of hard work and how it was applied to your women in the Marines.

Streeter: Well, I don't really know why you're surprised at that. I would have thought it was just something that came naturally.

Q: You think so, in this modern world, that it comes naturally?

Streeter: I wasn't in the modern world, my dear man. That was not a modern world. We were governed by the Articles for the Government of the Navy, known as "Rocks and Shoals," as you well know.

Oh, no. I don't quite follow you on that. I think I must have told you the story, that when I got promoted from a major to a lieutenant colonel, I had to take a physical exam, that being the rule, and it said on my physical exam, the examining doctor wrote, "Only lost two pounds in six months hard work."

That's where you must have got the idea that it was hard work. Well, of course it was hard work, but who the heck wasn't working hard? I mean, you worked till the job was done. And as a matter of fact, of course, I did comparaitvely little over time. I had friends in the Army, mostly in the Army, who were always being called back at night and Saturdays and Sundays and everything. We had alternate Saturdays off, in my office, and I seldom got one, about once in six weeks, because I was very likely to be out visiting some camp, on the weekend that would have been my weekend off, and so the assistant director would have to be on the job at headquarters. And I always felt I'd had the fun and she hadn't, so, I worked it out and let her keep her regular Saturdays off. So I guess I got a Saturday off about once in six weeks or so.

Q: So this philosophy of hard work really applied in your own particular case too.

Streeter: Well, yes, but I don't see why anybody's surprised. Everybody did what was needed. And I was not called back, I was never called back at night, and I think that the Marine Corps operated, not necessarily more efficiently, because I don't know what constraints it was under, but my friends in the Army were constantly being called back to headquarters sometimes.

No, it was pretty constant work, but I don't think it was particularly hard work, and I don't know what anybody expected, if not to work hard.

Q: You told me last time, in talking about your family, that you had very little leave during that whole period when you served there as director.

Streeter: Well, I might have had said so. I don't know if I told you why I didn't take it. I didn't take it because I thought if one of the boys was wounded or something, you know, if I could get to him, perhaps I could --

Q: One of your sons, you mean.

Streeter: Yes. Perhaps I'd be allowed to go to him, if I had leave coming to me. So I think I had very little actual leave, maybe one week during the whole three years. In fact, I had about six weeks accumulated unused leave. But that was my own choice.

Q: Now, I want to introduce another subject, because I understand from conversation with you off tape that the Marine system was quite different from the Navy, in terms of the women.

Mildred McAfee told me about her kaffee klatsche, her daily kaffee klatsches with women who were dispersed in various bureaus of the Navy, department and so forth, and it was her way of keeping informed as to what was going on in these various bureaus, and adding to her knowledge of the Navy as a total picture. Now, your system was somewhat different.

Streeter: Well, you've got to think of it that they were about five times bigger than we were.

Q: Yes.

Streeter: That made a considerable difference. And in effect, she was using the kaffee klatsches to which I occasionally came when invited as a staff. Well, we had the same general system at Headquarters Marine Corps, because in every division or department, we had a senior woman officer. Plans and Policies, Quartermaster, Discipline, Public Information, you name it, we had a senior woman officer, and I kept in close touch with all of them. But it was in one great big headquarters, and I either called them to come see me, or I went to see them. I didn't have a daily kaffee klatsche.

Q: And you did have in the Marines a system of what were called assistants for the Women's Reserve.

Streeter: Well, this was a strange and rather unorthodox thing. In the very first year, I think we had three women who had had special - well, they hadn't all had it, but they were appointed to be the senior women officers at some of the big camps, Camp Le Jeune, and Pendleton and San Diego, I think. There were more than three. There were four or five. And they were advisory capacity to the commanding general, same as I was advisory capacity to the head of the Division of Reserves at Headquarters. It was a good idea.

Q: They sent in official communications to you, did they?

Streeter: I don't think they did, at that particular time. This was in the very beginning, and eventually, a more widespread network grew up, in about the third year, the last year, where the senior woman officer, even in rather small post or station, would write a report. This of course was by order to the Commandant, which would make its way up to me. Now, this was not a report to me, directly. This was a report through channels, and of course I want to stress this, because it's very important in the Marine Corps to go through channels, and it meant that if a woman officer wanted to report something to me, she had to report it first to her commanding officer, and he would read it and he would okay it to go on to me. And unless he okayed it, it didn't go on to me. So this meant that she, of course, had to be specific and careful in what she said.

But it at least did allow for the fact that I couldn't possibly get around in person to visit all these places, and that if something came up in which she thought I might be helpful, if it reached me at Headquarters, actually what it meant was, inviting the attention of her commanding officer to the fact that it might be useful to report it to me. She did not ever go over the head of her commanding officer to me. And I think you have to stress this, because that is something that the Marine Corps never would tolerate.

I think it became useful in the end. Although it was slightly illogical from their point of view.

Well, haven't we about finished with the Marine Corps?

Q: Not exactly. Tell me about the Women's Band.

Streeter: Oh, the Women's Band, oh yes. Well, the Women's Band was a very fine outfit. Yes, Captain Santelman was the head of the Marine Corps Band at this time.

Q: He had had experience as a band leader.

Streeter: Oh, yes. Well, you know, the Marine Corps Band is a very expert band, and he came down --

Q: Oh, I was thinking it was a woman who --

Streeter: No, no, Captain Sandeman was the head of the Marine Corps Band. And he came down to Camp LeJeune along about October of '43, after we'd gotten started down there, and he came down to find out if there were people with sufficient musical training available, and to see what the chances were of putting together a Women's Band.

He was delighted. He came down to one of our Saturday reviews, and he thought they were wonderful and he thought the women were fine. He did select and sent somebody down to train the Women's Band, and they were awfully good. They were sort of the pride of the Marine Corps. They played for Saturday reviews, and they were sent around the country to play at recruiting things and at any special occasions. They were very well and favorably known, and they had a very fine spirit of their own. They were a little organization within an organization, and they still are. They come back to the reunions. Last time, two or three years ago, about half of them got back with half of their instruments and they put together a pretty good band, march.

Well, there was one of the musicians in the main band, the big Marine Corps Band with the barracks in Washington, who wrote a march for the Women Marines. That was fine. So they used to play that on all occasions.

Q: What is it called?

Streeter: "The March of the Women Marines." The leader eventually married, not the man who wrote that, but one of the musicians, and later on I think he played in the

Streeter #4 - 278

Philadelphia Symphony, so they were a good musical organization, and they had lots of pep, and along toward the end of the war, I was down at Camp LeJeune one time, and most people don't realize how low the manpower pool was, but by what was our third year, fifth year really of the war, they were taking 17 year old boys as officer candidates. Now, they'd been taking them in the aviation section for some time, because they could fly like bats out of hell, though they were awful on the ground.

Q: Dare devils.

Streeter: Yes. Well, they were a lot of problems to me on the ground. They'd get off on a little air strip somewhere -- of course there were no girls around except the enlisted women -- so they would take off their bars and have a dance, which of course I knew nothing about officially. There being certain rules about fratrenization. But I didn't see what else they could do so I didn't pay much attention.

Well, anyhow, they'd had 17 year olds as fliers, but they had not had them in the land forces.

Even the Marine Corps thought that trying to train 17 year olds to be line officers was pretty rough. And so they didn't put them at once into officer training school. They were officer training "aspirants", and they put in several weeks down at Camp LeJeune being aspirants, before they really even got into officer training. And of course they had more pep than anybody else in the Marine Corps by that time. The rest of us were pretty tired. So they wanted, for their Saturday review, they wanted the snappies to outfit in the way of music that they could get at Camp LeJeune, so they used to have their review with the Women Marines Band.

Q: What uniforms did the Women's Marine Band wear?

Streeter: The same as ours. We didn't have any fancy uniforms during the war.

Q: That white uniform was pretty fancy.

Streeter: It was very plain. Nothing fancy about it except the gold buttons. But in the beginning of his war, Hitler said, "Give me an army of 17 year olds and I'll lick the world."

That's true. They're so anxious to show that they're men and all. And very sad, really. I thought it was a little sad to see them down at Camp LeJeune. But most of them didn't get into the fighting.

Q: Tell me a little about those Saturday reviews. You participated in them largely in Washington?

Streeter #4 - 280

Streeter: No, they didn't have them regularly in Washington. They didn't have them regularly. They had them on occasion.

Q: But they made big occasions of that time.

Streeter: I don't think they appeared publicly much of any. We had one review of the Headquarters Battalion once for General Waller, before he went off to Hawaii, because he'd been sort of patron saint of the women, and we had, at the time of our anniversary each year, we'd have a review. But we didn't - they were working. Their bosses didn't like them to take off to march.

Q: Well, the net result of all this, and all the effort you put forward in it, was that you were awarded the Legion of Merit. Tell me about that.

Streeter: Well, that was I thought very nice of them. I wasn't awarded it till after I was demobilized, so it never got pinned on me, because by that time I was in civies. But, yes. I was awarded it, at the request of the Commandant with a very nice citation which I prize highly, although it does embarrass me to some extent, because it sounds as if I did everything, you know, when after all the 19,000 other women did quite a lot.

Q: There were only two such awards given, were there not?

Streeter: Well, to me at that time and to my successor, all my successors. The colonels who have been directors of women have all received it at the end of their term of office. But this was the first one, of course. And then in addition, when I did get out, General Vandergrift wrote me a very nice letter of appreciation, both of which I have out here. And of course I was very pleased that the Marine Corps was satisfied with what I'd done. But as I say, it was mostly the other 19,000 that did it.

Q: Have you been at many of the reunions? They do have reunions, do they not?

Streeter: Oh, yes. The Women Marines Association. I've been to several of them. There was one in San Francisco in '48 and there was one in Boston, not '48, it was '68, and there was one in Boston not so long ago that I went to. I don't go to all of them any more. But they're quite active still. And of course the Marine Corps is wonderful, because it's quite true that once a Marine, always a Marine, and when they discovered last winter that I'd had an unexpected operation and was staying in the hospital for a while, I got more cards, more flowers, more messages of one sort and another, all the way from the Commandant down to the little recruits at Camp LeJeune. And all these plants that you see around have survived. The flowering plants haven't lasted this long. But the others have survived. The people in Hawaii sent me a box this long of those great red flowers.

Q: Anthurium.

Streeter: Yes. And the people in the camps, the posts and stations, sent them to me, and of course they don't know me. I mean all the Women Marines of World War II are all long since out - well, not all, but -

Q: They're somewhat mature at this point, aren't they?

Streeter: Yes. It's thirty odd years after the end of the war, what is it, '33? So they're out. For the first time the senior woman officer, who's now a brigadier general, and not Director of Women Marines - there is no such thing as Director of Women Marines any more, in the Marine Corps -

Q: It's been incorporated into the personnel.

Streeter: It's been incorporated. She, as it happens, is Director of Public Information. It's her job. And this feeling, which I think was very important, certainly during World War II, probably of diminishing importance, that it was a good thing to have some senior woman, particularly looking after, looking out for the interests of the women, has become - now we're all integrated thoroughly and there's no need for it anymore.

Q: It's a unisex sort of thing today.

Streeter: Oh, yes.

Q: I want to read this on the tape, in connection with what Mrs. Streeter has been saying about her illness, when she was confined to the Morristown Memorial Hospital, this past winter, and how the Marine Corps reacted. This is a personal delivery message, dated February 15, 1970, to Colonel Ruth Streeter, U.S. Marine Corps, Retired, in the Morristown Memorial Hospital.

"Dear Colonel Streeter: I've just learned of your hospitalization, and on behalf of your many friends in the Marine Corps, I send sincere wishes to you for a rapid recovery. Your many years of devoted service to the Marine Corps, and your loyal support since your separation from its active roles, are certainly a testimony to your esprit de corps and patriotism to this great country. Our concern and prayers are extended to you, during this difficult time. But we also add our optimistic hope that your condition will soon be greatly improved. Sincerely, Louis H. Wilson, General, U.S. Marine Corps, Commandant of the Marine Corps."

I might add another citation here. In addition to the

dispatch from General Wilson, at the time of Mrs. Streeter's illness in the hospital, she also received several charming little things from some of the enlisted Marines –

Streeter: The little recruits.

Q: – recruits down at Parris Island, yes, "Get Well" cards they're called, signed by a number of the girls. Then here is one which is truly delightful. It's labeled "A Get Well Thought, from a highly motivated, truly dedicated, rough and tough." What is that?

Streeter: Oh, private, I don't know –

Q: Private No. 2 A.

Streeter: Oh, Platoon 2 A. That's the platoon.

Q: Then inside the cover is a little verse:
"The sun shines brighter,
Each and every day gets lighter,
Our platoon is strong and swell,
Wishing you a quick Get Well. Respectfully," and at the bottom, it's the name of Theresa Ford is attached and it says, "motivated by Thersa Ford." Perfectly charming things, as remembrances to her in the hospital, and I'm sure they helped in bringing about her recovery.

Streeter: They certainly did. And this is one of the instances that shows how the Marines live up to their motto, that "once a Marine, always a Marine," because neither the Commandant nor obviously the recruits have ever seen me or known me at all, and the top and the bottom of the Marine Corps roster both went out of their way to send me best wishes, and so did innumerable Marines in between, so that I really couldn't do anything less than get well, with all those good wishes. I was really very much touched by all their taking an interest.

Q: Now we want to talk about a few of the military connections which you maintained after you left the Marine Corps in December, 1945. I note that you became a member of the New Jersey Veterans Council, and you served there during the years 1946-53. Tell me about that. What did it entail?

Streeter: Well, that led eventually to one of the most interesting experiences of my life. It was a natural thing to do, I think, for Governor Driscoll to appoint me to this council. We were very busy at the time in the state of New Jersey, as in many other states, supplementing the help which returned veterans received from the GI Bill of Rights. Housing, for instance, was one of the chief problems. We had to put up temporary housing, in for instance the big park in the center of Newark, and in many other places we had to provide temporary housing. So many of these men of course promptly got married when they got home and had families, and there simply was not that much accommodation for them, so that was one of the first things that the Veterans Services Council did.

And then in addition, it helped with educational rights, and all of the things that the GI Bill covered.

Q: How many served on this council?

Streeter: I think there were six or seven of us.

Q: You were pretty busy, with all these issues.

Streeter: Well, we had a staff, of course. We had quite a staff. Because we had offices, local offices where the veterans could easily go to inquire about their rights and get their necessary forms filled out and all that.

Q: Were you the only woman on the council then?

Streeter: Yes.

Q: You were.

Streeter: I often was. They used to begin the meetings, "Mrs. Streeter and gentlemen."

Well, this really was quite a job, and the state of New Jersey I think was very helpful in supplementing and making connections with the federal grants.

Q: Was this true of other states as well, or was it peculiar to New Jersey?

Streeter: Oh, I think it must have been true of all the states practically. But there was one thing we did not do in the beginning in New Jersey, and of course there was a later demand for it, and that was to have a state bonus, flag payments, to the veterans. This bill was passed by the legislature and sent to a referendum, to see if the people of New Jersey wanted to do this.

Q: They had to pay the bill.

Streeter: Because they had to pay the bill. And because I was on the Veterans Services Council, there was a meeting in Morristown and I was asked to speak about this, and go into some detail about it, so that people would know what a sensible vote would be.

Of course, because I had those connections, I was able to get statistics, and I made an effort to do so and to go quite thoroughly into the whole problem. I explained exactly what the Bill of Rights covered. It covered in the first place any possible services to the men who had been killed or to their families. Their children for instance had certain preferences. Then of course to the ones who were injured, many of whom were still in hospitals and others of whom had disability payments. In both those groups, of course, anything that could be done for them, everybody was in favor of doing.

Then there was the whole further group, which was of course the majority of the men who came back, not disabled, but having lost three or four or sometimes five years out of their lives, while they were in the service and other people of course were working in civilian occupations, were getting good jobs, were getting good pay, and these men were behind the eight ball when they came back. They had lost time and training. So the government, this is the federal GI Bill that I'm talking about now, the government became the partner of the veterans in making opportunities open to them that probably they would not have had if they had not gone to war. The government put up the money, the veteran put up the work and the effort to make the money effective. This is the GI Bill of Rights, for instance, on which so many veterans went to college and some to high school, some to graduate school. Anyhow, that was one of the big advantages. Many of them would have have gone there at all, except for this special payment which was made to them and enabled them to do it.

There was agricultural training. There were grants made by the government for money to buy houses or money to buy farms, and to go into small businesses. There was a whole series of advantages given to veterans whereby the government paid and they made the effort, and this was to enable them to catch up for all the years that they had been away.

I expressed being heartily in favor of all of these.

But then I said that I was not in favor of paying the veterans a flat bonus. I think the amount was supposed to be $500, to any veterans who had served overseas, and $250 to any veteran who had not gotten out of this country. And I said that I didn't think you could put a price on patriotism. No money was worth what a lot of them had been through and why would you say $500 and not $5000 or something like that? I thought the whole idea was wrong, the whole emphasis was wrong, and I personally was opposed to this measure which was coming up for referendum.

Well, I knew, of course, that this would bring down considerable wrath on my head. I'd taken the trouble of sending a transcript of my speech to the local paper so that it would get to them in advance and they would have a chance to print it fully, which they did. Then I waited for the storm to break, but I didn't think that it would break quite so quickly or quite so heavily as it did.

The next night, I had an appointment in New York,

which I preceded to go to, not realizing that Governor Driscoll of New Jersey was going to be in Morristown that evening and was going to make a public speech.

Well, he did come. The Legion excoriated me, said I'd insulted the memory of the dead, was absolutely furious, put the governor on the spot, and generally made a mess of things. And I of course was very annoyed when I heard about it, that I hadn't been here to answer their questions myself. But at least I did answer them in the paper, and I wrote the governor at once and apologized for not being here and offered my resignation.

Well, I heard nothing from him. Several days went by. So finally I called his office and said, "Did the governor get my letter?"

"Oh, yes," they said.

"Well," I said, "I handed in my resignation. What's he going to do about it?"

"Oh," they said, "he isn't going to do anything about it."

"Well, what did he say about it?"

They said, "He just laughed."

That was Governor Driscoll for you. And of course then I was sorrier than ever that I hadn't been here, and had let him get in hot water in my home town without being there to defend him.

Q: Did you bring up the question of whether it was a waste

of public funds or not?

Streeter: Oh, no. Oh, no. I just said you couldn't put a price on patriotism. Well, that was just the beginning. Then you should have seen my mail, practically all of it anonymous. I thought I was reasonably used to four letter words, but I certainly learned many that I'd never heard before, addressed to me. Scurrilous letters. They really were. I saved them for a while, because I thought it was good for me, if I ever had a swelled head, to just go and look at them again.

But then about one in twenty were different letters. One, for instance, said, "I'm a small shop keeper. I have been threatened by American Legion people, that unless I vote for the referendum, my store will be boycotted. I'm afraid to say these things but I'm glad that you said them."

One of the most touching of all was badly misspelled and rather scrawly writing, but it said, "I have had two sons in the Army in Germany, and they say you are just right and I am to write and tell you so." That was the most encouraging one I had.

Well, time went on, and this furor about me went up and down the whole state of New Jersey. It wasn't just in Morristown or Morris County. It became a very hot issue. And you know what happened? The referendum was overwhelmingly defeated. It was so badly defeated the first time it was put up that the legislature has never even put a referendum again, and the state of New Jersey is one of only two or three in the United States which had no soldiers' bonus. No state bonus. To this day.

And the point of that is that the families of the soldiers themselves must have done it, because they would have been an overwhelming majority, if they had voted in favor of it. The fact that they voted against it - it was not the non-service people, it was the service men and their families. And this is one of the most interesting experiences I have had in my life, and I don't know whether it shows that if you, if one person or a small group of people will take a stand, that other people of the same cast of mind will coalesce around them, or not. I think it's very chancy. I think that quite often it does not happen. But it happened this time and it happened to overshelmingly that the issue has never been raised again.

Q: Did you have any personal comment from Driscoll?

Streeter: Oh, I don't think so. He just said, "Oh nonsense, you get in hot water any time you're in public life." "You get used to it, that's all."

No, he was a good governor, and of course, I was very pleased that he took it that way.

Q: How did your husband react to all these little brickbats you got in the mail?

Streeter: Oh, he didn't care. This was my headache. If I wanted to go get myself in hot water, that was my hard luck.

I did want to tell you about that, because it was one of the most interesting experiences of my life, and I've always wondered how far it could be used as something that might be repeated under similar circumstances or not. I can only say I think it's very chancy. It's only - you see, the overwhelming swell was the demand for it, and how could anybody have guessed that with the tremendous demand for it, that the thing would be voted down by a silent majority, apparently, who were all families of the men who'd been in service.

Q: Rather a beguiling thing, to have ready money, ready cash to spend.

Streeter: I know it.

Q: Which is what would happen. It was spent sometimes overnight.

Streeter: Yes, that's what would have happened. And well,

Streeter #4 - 294

you know, they just rose above it somehow. And this was within a year or two of the end of the war.

Well --

Q: Were there any other things on the Veterans Council that had significance?

Streeter: I think not particularly, no. It was the usual run of things, just to expedite things from time to time.

Q: Then you belonged to the United States Defense Advisory Council for Women in the Service.

Streeter: Well, that was kind of honorary. Advisory councils are always kind of honorary. Nobody has to take your advice.

Q: Did they ask for your advice?

Streeter: Oh, we had meetings from time to time, yes. And it was very friendly and very nice. Tell you one thing that did happen, that was rather memorable. We were having a meeting in the Pentagon, at the time that General Eisenhower was retired, as General of the Armies, to run for President, of course. He came to the Pentagon. He came into the room where we all were, and spoke a few words to us, and then, we all went to one of the offices on the front of the

Pentagon, which overlooked the little terrace where the retirement ceremony was to take place. So we saw it all.

He arrived in his car, with the flags, the five star flag and the American flag, and then, the troops, representative detachments from the various services, were lined up on the grass, on the terrace, and his orders were read, and he was retired.

Then he left in his car and the flags were cased. You know how you case a flag, put a cover over it.

Q: Yes. How could he retire as a five star general? I thought they were always on duty.

Streeter: Well, I don't know. But they did. Well, he had to be. He had to get out of that before he became President.

Q: Yes. I guess he was out temporarily but it was restored as a status afterwards.

Streeter: Yes. This must have all been legally attended to.

Well, as I say, I was not very active on that but it was an interesting committee.

Q: Were the other former directors on it too?

Streeter #4 - 296

Streeter: I think they were all on it. I don't remember how many of them were there that day.

Q: Then another thing, which is listed here, is that in 1975 you were presented by the Air Force with a placque in connection with the Cheney Award.

Streeter: Oh, yes. Well, have I told you about that, about the Cheney Award?

Q: Yes, you had told me about the Cheney Award, about how you and your mother set it up in memory of your brother who was killed in World War I. But in '75 you were given a placque in recognition of your service in connection with this award. Now, what is that?

Streeter: Well, I'll show it to you.

Q: Yes, but explain it to me, your service in connection with it.

Streeter: Well, my mother and I, as I think I told you in an earlier interview, had taken the war risk life insurance that my brother had made out to both of us, and had set it up as an award in the Air Force, which has been given now for well over 50 years, and they have complete control over it. There's a medal, large sized medal and a check that goes to each recipient. It's for courage and self sacrifice in flying conditions, not for action against the enemy. They think very highly of it, and we have felt that it was a very tangible and very satisfying commemoration of my brother.

One time, the wife of an Air Force general said to me, "How fortunate you are. You have a continual contact with courage." And so it is, year after year.

So General McConnell, who was chief of staff of the Air Force at that time, did present me in 1975 with this tablet thanking me for that connection.

Q: And I would think, for the fact that you added to this sum of money from time to time, didn't you?

Just as the tape ended, you told me that the money was well invested so it grew, because I had intimated that you had added to the sum for the Cheney Award through the years. Now you were about to tell me that just recently, in June, the chief of staff of the Air Force came to call on you.

Streeter: He did indeed. He is a new chief of staff. The former chief of staff, whom I had known, General David C. Jones, is now Chairman of the Joint Chiefs of Staff, and this General Allen I think is the first chief of staff of the Air

Streeter #4 - 298

Force who did not serve in World War II. All the services now have pretty well outgrown the high ranking officers that had served in World War II. I believe the Marine Corps is the only one that still has a top officer with that experience, because it's getting to be a long time ago now.

Q: Inadvertently that dates us, doesn't it.

Streeter: It dated me long ago. And General Allen is very, very nice. And when I had written him that I would not be able to come down to Washington in the hot weather for the presentation of the award, he was kind enough to say, if I couldn't come to Washington, he'd come to Morristown, because he'd like very much to meet me.

So he tried to get in about a month ago, and it was a perfectly horrible day, fog and rain and wind, so fortunately he didn't try to come in, but he said he would try again, and he came in about three weeks ago, flew into Morristown Airport, and I met him with the mayor of Morristown, and the mayor duly presented him with the keys to the town, to the township, and then, I took him up here to my little house and we just relaxed, and he and his aide, Major Polling, and talked about old times and had a very delightful visit. That makes me feel all over again, what a real pleasure and great satisfaction it has been to have this relationship with the Air Force. The things the men have done are absolutely startlingly courageous; many of them, several of them I'm afraid have lost their lives, but many of them have saved lives too by what they've done.

Q: We're coming back to Morristown after World War II, after this three year tour of duty you had in Washington, D.C. Do you want to take up the story at that point?

Streeter: Well, I now resume my two track life. I found, as I think that probably all returning servicemen felt, that an adjustment was a little difficult in the beginning, even though it was something we'd been looking forward to for a long time. When we went in to the armed forces, it was a complete change from anything we'd known before. But we had lots of company. Everybody around us was doing the same thing, and when you come out, you come out alone, to make your readjustment alone, and this is sometimes more difficult.

I think it's an extraordinary tribute to the people who did come back, that so many of them have made the adjustment so well, and it's only a few who have had any great trouble.

As far as I was concerned, of course I was delighted to be home with my husband and my daughter, and more, unutterably thankful really that our three sons were not ever scratched. They all came home. They were of the age when they were expendable, and all in jobs where they were expendable, and as luck would have it, none of them were scratched. None of them had battle fatigue or anything like that. They were all perfectly well and very glad to be home in their turn too.

So I've always felt that whatever Providence there is certainly watched over us, and I wouldn't know why they should have watched over us any more than over anybody else, but we're just grateful that that's what happened.

They all then began to return to their, what would become their usual lives. Our oldest boy Frank was by that time a lieutenant commander in the Navy. He'd been on destroyer duty, in the Gulf of Mexico, and in the Pacific. He'd been at Okinawa, which was a miserable place to be on a destroyer, with the kamikazes -

Q: Was he on a picket ship?

Streeter: He was on something there. Yes, he was on a destroyer. I suppose it was a picket ship.

Q: He probably took his turn as a picket ship.

Streeter: Our losses from the kamikazes were far greater I think than people mostly realize. He came back, and he is now an assistant to Mr. Jock Whitney. He's in charge of his personal affairs in New York. Mr. Whitney of course was ambassador to England at one time and is a very well known New York man.

Our second son Henry had always intended to be a lawyer, so he no sooner got back, having graduated from Harvard on an accelerated course, before he also became a destroyer man - he got back and went to Harvard Law School. He was the last of the boys to get back, because his ship spent six months after the war, the winter months, on the China Sea, sweeping mines, of all the difficult and dangerous and unpleasant types of job - and then he was skipper of a very decrepit destroyer that he had to bring back across the Pacific, and luckily they didn't run into any gales. He said it was stuck together with chewing gum and string.

He is now partner in Ropes and Gray, one of the big law firms in Boston.

Our third boy, Tommy, who had been a sergeant in the Army in the OSS, had been out in the China-Burma-India Theatre for some time. He'd flown the Hump into China several times, and he was in communications in the OSS.

He came back and went into the stock brokerage business, which must have been about as lively, I should think, if not to say as dangerous as flying the Hump.

Anyhow, they all got married very shortly and began to produce children and grandchildren and this was fine, as far as my husband and I were concerned. We finally had seventeen grandchildren of our own, with four step-grandchilren.

Our daughter Lil was the one who had the largest family. She had the four step-grandchildren, and her first husband and she had four more children, and he died in a swimming accident. She married again later and had four more children, so she had eight of her own and four step-children, making twelve in all.

She is an extraordinary character. Her first husband was a very fine boy who had been in the Navy, on destroyer duty too - actually he lied about his health when he went into the service, because he had had epilepsy, and they had trepanned his skull in the hope of relieving pressure on the brain to cure him, and they put in a silver plate. What happened was, he was swimming in the surf one day off Fire Island and was apparently rolled by the surf, and must have hit his head on a clam shell or stone or something, right on the silver shield and it just gave way.

That was her first family. Then she married Dr. Britton Chance who is a scientist, a very fine scientist. He's head of the scientific foundation at the University of Pennsylvania. He's a biophysicist, and he has international connections, and is a brilliant man. So we have interesting in-laws and interesting grandchildren, and we now have three great-grandchildren, three little girls. So that takes care of our family and their postwar activities.

Meanwhile, all this time, my husband had been devoting himself to his book collection, which he started, which he began giving his full attention to after he retired from active business in December, 1939. He had always had some interest in it, from the time we were first married, along about 1920, but then, along came the Depression, and things got worse and worse for everybody, including ourselves. It was a miserable time, and I have reflected sometimes that as between wars and depressions, the effect of depressions is so much worse, on what it does to people.

Now, this sounds extraordinary, because war kills them, of course. Depressions don't necessarily kill. But they destroy them just as thoroughly, because these people, mostly men, who have always been self respecting, who have been proud of doing a job, good job, who have been proud of supporting their families and giving them opportunities, suddenly found there were no jobs.

It wasn't that they weren't adequately doing their jobs, it was simply that there were no jobs. And this did something rather awful to their self esteem, their self respect. I don't know what the answer to depressions is. I don't think anybody has found it. But I know it's a dreadful thing.

There was a time when Tom didn't have a job, and you know, we mortgaged the house, we raised what money we could. Then he was fortunate enough to have a job, and we managed to pay our way through as we went along. But I can easily know from experience how it must have been for people who weren't that lucky and who had to go on month after month, year after year, watching all their accumulated protection dissolve, and feeling unwanted and unneeded.

Of course, the thing that rescued the United States from this Depression was the onset of World War II. The factories began making ammunition and arms for the allies, the English, the French and the others. Therefore more jobs opened up. Then in due time jobs opened up to arm our own country. That is not a cure for depressions that I recommend. But that was, rather than any methods that were attempted by the government, with the best intentions in the workd, but not very effectively - that was what brought us out of that Depression.

As I think about it again sometimes, now that we're all talking about depressions or recessions or something or other - what we've done since then, of course, is the dole. Whatever you call it, welfare or anything else. We pay people to keep them from starving.

Of course, you should. You've got to keep them from starving. The theory is that they work for what you pay them. This unfortunately is not always borne out by fact, and generations are growing up whose idea of work is not anything that anybody would pay two cents for. And this is very bad.

Again, I don't know the answer. I certainly hope that another war is not the answer. We've been trying through

Social Security and through CETA grants and through all kinds of ways of distributing money to see that it gets to the people who need it and keeps them afloat. But it certainly is not building a sturdy self-reliant country out of us, or a sturdy self-reliant and responsible citizenry. We just don't know exactly what it *is* doing to our people.

Q: Another such thing as the Great Depression would find us in quite a different situation. I wonder what the results would be? The family as a unit is no longer as it was. And now, you have both men and women employed, so you'd have women thrown out of work too. What would be the result?

Streeter: Well, nobody knows. We tried to cure the Great Depression, the 1929 Depression, by cutting down. Well, I don't think we cured it.

Q: Then we applied public works, all that kind of thing.

Streeter: Yes.

Q: PWA.

Streeter: Now, we don't try cutting down at all. We just try paying out. And with no adequate standards of work supplied in return for the pay. That's the trouble.

The one good thing that worked well in the Great Depression was the so-called Civilian Conservation Corps. And the reason it worked well was because it was really more or less under Army discipline, although they did not have Army discipline, but it was under the direction of Army officers, and they took these young boys from the cities. They took them right out of the cities, where they had bad habits, bad companions, bad ways of spending their time, and took them out to the National Parks and to other places in the country where they weren't distracted, and they put them to work and they worked them hard. And when those boys finished their time in the Civilian Conservation Corps, they knew how to work. They had no difficulty getting jobs, if there were any jobs at all, because they were reliable competent workmen, with an idea of what a good day's work meant. And this has not been done at the present time under those terms. It probably would not work. There's much less wild land to take them out of the cities and send them to, for one thing. And there are other complications too. But that was the only plan which really produced good results. The rest produced in various ways. Some things in public works were done. Sometimes they were done well, sometimes not. And otherwise there was a great deal of leaf raking.

Now, I must say a word or two for leaf raking. If you live in the country, you know that disposing of leaves is a big problem. At the moment locally we're having a great fight, as to what's to be done with the leaves, because we're not allowed to burn them any more, and the thing about leaf raking was that anybody could rake leaves. You didn't have to be a skilled workman to rake leaves. So a lot of people who were not skilled workmen were taken care of by leaf raking. I don't know what the equivalent of it is nowadays, but, all I mean is that the Depression was the word for it: everybody was terribly depressed. You don't get depressed in war time. Somehow or other, you're much more worried, you have much more to worry about, but you also have a rising tide of determination which carries you through.

Q: Almost exhilaration.

Streeter: Yes. And people all worked together. Practically the only thing they say is, "What did he or she do to help win the war?" They don't say, "Did you ever get drunk?" or anything like that. It doesn't seem to count any more.

Whether this country, after all the trouble about Vietnam, would pull itself together in the face of a real threat against the continued independence of the United States, I don't think anybody can tell.

What has happened to the stamina, the soul of the country, we don't know. And we can't tell.

Part of it is the effect of long time unemployment,

several generations sometimes in one family, a habit of unemployment, and part of it is the aftermath of the Vietnam War, which was a war that certainly did us more harm than it did anybody else, I think, and just how the young people feel, I don't know.

I must say that I don't lose too much sleep over the South Vietnamese. If they'd done a little better fighting, they wouldnt' have had all these boat people now. But of course what's happening is, the boat people aren't South Vietnamese. They're Chinese. But the Chinese of course were living in Vietnam at the time. It's a very confused situation.

Well, I didn't mean to get off on that track too much, but --

Q: Very interesting digression, however.

Streeter: Well, you see, I was on the State Relief Council in the middle of the Depression, and we did our darnedest, but we did it largely by squeezing, not paying any more than we could help for what was done. Now we've gone to the opposite extreme for many years now, and we spent money without asking very much in return.

I don't think that either way is very effective. It's poulticing the boil, that's all.

Well, to come back to my own family. During the time

that the boys and I were off at war, and Tom and Lil had been keeping each other company, which they did very effectively - they went up to the Adirondacks to the Ausable Club, where we had been some years previously, and this was an idea that I had, when I began to wonder what they would do in the summer time. Because it's a delightful place. They always have lots of young people who love to go camping and hiking in the woods and all, and they also have older people who have done that and are perfectly willing to sit around and have a cocktail in the evening and play a little golf and disport themselves in more mild forms of exercise.

So they went up every summer and they had a very fine time. Then of course Lil was in school in the winter, and --

Q: Did they visit you in Washington very frequently?

Streeter: No, they never did.

Q: They never did. You had an apartment there?

Streeter: I had an apartment, yes.

Q: Where were you?

Streeter: Oh, I was on California Street -

Q: Right off Connecticut?

Streeter: Yes, right off Connecticut there. What was the number? Twenty-one something, I think. The Brighton. Do you know the Brighton?

Q: Yes, I know the Brighton.

Streeter: The Brighton. That's where I was. And I had a car, and I took General Denig and Colonel Towle to work every morning, and --

Q: Had a car pool then.

Streeter: Had a car pool, yes. Sure. The General contributed his parking lot, which was convenient. We wouldn't have had one within half a mile, probably. And we provided transportation.

Well, so, most of the time that we were all away, Tom having retired a year or two previously from active business was concentrating on his first love which was history and book collecting. And he made a whole new career for himself for the last twenty-five years of his life. He had a librarian and he had a couple of secretaries. People used to say, "Isn't it fortunate that your husband has a hobby?"

I said, "A hobby? You don't understand, this is a big business."

He really went at it that way. He became a member,

often president, of literary societies such as the Grolier Club and the Bibliographical Society of America, and he was treasurer of the New York Historical Society, and he belonged to the Walpole Society and he was a friend of practically every historical library in the country, I should think. He also, at this time, published some books.

The first one was his history of Texas. The very first one was called *Americana Beginnings*. That was a small book of carefully selected interesting books which he did for a meeting of the Roswitha Society, and then he really spent years writing a bibliography of Texas, to 1845, that is to say until the Mexican American War, from the beginning until then.

Q: Did this mean extensive traveling in Texas?

Streeter: Well, he had gone to Texas, you see, as a young man, in pursuit of oil, and he had become very much interested in Texas, because as you know, for eight years it was an independent republic. Not a part of the United States at all. And it had a fascinating history, and he was a collector by nature and by habit and by wish, and so he had formed a very good Texas collection, most of which he later sold to Yale, where it fitted very neatly between two other collections of Texas books, so that altogether Yale has a very fine extensive collection of them. And he published these volumes, and a bibliography is a very time consuming thing, especially the way he did it, because he would write a note about each book of any importance, not only located where the copies were and descriptions of the books, but he would write a note on them, and he tried to keep it short. Of course it's much more difficult to write a brief note than it is to write a lengthy note. And so this took him a lot of time, but it was the sort of thing that he thoroughly enjoyed doing.

After he had done that, then he began to catalogue the rest of his library. He had sold the Texas books to Yale. And his own library began with discoveries, first books in every state in the Union, and he wanted to have that sold at auction after his death. He was very specific about this. He had sold his Texas collection as a unit, but he said he did not want to sell the rest of his collection as a unit, because then it was frozen for all time. If he sold it to some university or something like that, nobody else could have the pleasure of owning it. So he wanted to have it auctioned, and have everybody have a whack at it. He even provided, knowing that eventually they would run out of money to buy at it, he provided that after the necessary fees and all had been covered, that certain grants should be made to these special libraries that would be interested. So this of course engendered a good deal of competition, and it took - the auctions were held in seven units, and it took three and a half years.

Tom died in 1965. The first auction was in the fall of 1966, and it took three and a half years, one auction every six months, so there were two a year, and they went very well. I think the gross amount was something over $3,100,000. Of course the net amount was very much less, and a considerable part of that had been given away also, but it came at a time, before inflation had driven up the price of objets d'art and specialities, to the ridiculous heights that they're at now, people buy them for investments now, but they were much higher than they had previously been. Part of this I think was due to the careful documentation that Tom had given them, and because he knew all the dealers and all the collectors and they knew what he had, and they knew that eventually it would come on the market. So this was very successful. Of course it took a long time. I was one of the executors. Doc O'Connor was the other, and we had three book dealers who were advisors to us, and we worked very hard on it for all those years, with the Parke-Bernet people, to get the catalogues, and I'll show you the catalogues out here presently.

Q: Were you sorry to see it dispersed?

Streeter: No, because what would I have done with it for heaven's sake? I knew something, Tom talked with me about it of course, and frequently discussed a lot of these things with me. I always said, like a doctor's wife who always tells you that the doctor never tells her about his patients, I always said I couldn't understand book collecting, and of course you can't unless you make it a real specialty, but you can get a pretty good grasp of the overall picture just from listening to all these people talk for twenty-five years. So we all got along very well, together, and worked very happily at it.

After the collection was catalogued and was sent to New York, then I moved from the big house into the little cottage where I live now. And the big house was torn down, mostly because none of the children wanted to come back to this neighborhood. It's far too big for me and far too big for most people to run in these days, and so I thought it would be better to just take it down, than to see it perhaps run downhill, be sold or rented to somebody who would not take care of it.

Q: But you retained the land.

Streeter: I'm right on the same land. I'm only about 100 yards away from it.

So, that takes pretty well care of our family.

Q: That's the family. But you have engaged in various other things outside of –

Streeter: There was one more thing I should say about the family, but I have to skip a generation, and that's why - skip two generations, in fact. That's why I overlooked it momentarily.

This has to do with our grandson, Thomas W. Streeter II.

Q: He's the son of Thomas?

Streeter: Son of Tommy. He was at college in Texas, Rice College in Texas when the Vietnam War broke out. And he and his father talked the situation over. First he decided he would go in the ROTC. It used to be said, for the people in the early days of the Vietnam War, nobody had thought anybody was going to fight any more after World War II until we ran into Korea, and the Korean War of course was a good old fashioned war. Somebody just marched over the border and there you were. So that rather obviously needed to be stopped, if it was possible to do so, or else it was going to get to be a habit, and the South Koreans were willing to fight, and so that was at least held to half Korea, was conquered and stayed to the present day, but the other half remained independent.

Well, in the early days, it looked as if Vietnam was going to be another Korea. But it was a very different sort of situation. In the first place, it was much more difficult to defend because it was mostly swamp and jungle, very short coast line. Korea, you see, three-quarters of it was coast line, could be defended by the Navy, and Vietnam had to be largely defended by the Army and also the Air Force, of course.

It was a much more difficult war to wage militarily speaking, and the South Vietnamese didn't seem to care particularly whether the North Vietnamese beat them or not. The upper level was so corrupt that you couldn't blame the lower level people for not particularly being interested in fighting.

Anyhow it became really a disaster to everybody concerned, and particularly to us, I think, because it was not the kind of war that anybody could be very enthusiastic about.

But for the young men of that time, it was a problem, and many of them of course ducked it, stayed in college largely was the idea. Some went to Canada. Some just, you know, got out of the way. But young Tom talked it over with his father and felt that that was not the way he wanted to act. So he went in the ROTC.

Then he became a little disillusioned with the ROTC, decided that instead of waiting to graduate and become an officer, he would just up and enlist. So he did. He enlisted as a private in the 101st Airborne Division. In due time of course he was sent to Vietnam and in due time he was sent into the jungle, and he was about -- they did a six months tour in the jungle mostly, and he was in about four months, I should think, when one day they were ordered to recapture a fire base in the jungle which they had once captured.

Of course, that was another thing that used to go wrong. We would capture some place and fortify it, and then we'd decide, somebody at headquarters would decide that wasn't really necessary, and they'd evacuate it. Then somebody else at headquarters would decide that after all it was important, we'd better go back and take it again. And of course, the North Vietnamese people always knew where we were going to come before we got there, so they were always lying in wait. That didn't make it any more easy to recapture.

So these planes would land, for the 101st Airborne to get out, and of course it was like landing on a beach. Until you got out of the landing vessel, you were very vulnerable because you all had to get out through a small space. And the same when you got out of a helicopter, you're very vulnerable till you can find a foxhole and get under some sort of cover.

So of course the Viets let fly at them, as they were getting out, and Tommy got out all right, into a foxhole, but the soldier who was carrying their hand radio dropped it, out in the open, and I don't know if he was wounded or not, he probably was; and so Tommy jumped out of the foxhole, ran out and collected it, and ran back again, and fortunately was not wounded, but he was given the Bronze Star for that.

Then he eventually came home all right, so he got married and now has two little girls, is a lawyer in Texas.

Q: He was not injured?

Streeter: He was not injured, no. Well, he was not injured on that occasion. He was not wounded. But later on, he was injured - talking about coincidences, as we have several times, in this story, later on he was on patrol in the jungle. And of course they carry a great heavy weight on their shoulders, you know, and he tripped over a root or something in the jungle, fell down and pulled a tendon, so that he was very lame. He could not get around at all, and finally he did manage to get to a clearing, and they sent for one of the air rescue helicopters, which came over and let down what they call a jungle penetrator for him, which is a seat on the end of a wire rope. So he got strapped onto the seat and then they winch him up. This is when they can't come down, of course, to land. And they carried him out to the Navy hospital ship Sanctuary.

And the coincidence is that because of my connection with the Cheney Award, a number of the people in the air rescue business in Vietnam had done just this sort of thing, and had gotten the Cheney Award for it, when they rescued people who were actually under attack from the Vietnamese. Well, Tommy wasn't under attack but he certainly wouldn't have gotten out of the jungle any other way, I guess, except by being air lifted out.

So the bread I'd cast upon the waters in one respect came back to me that way. And the other had to do with the USS Sanctuary, because the Colonial Dames, of which I was a member and president at one time, had raised a great deal of money really to give extra supplies to the Red Cross girls on two of the Navy hospital ships, the Sanctuary and the Repose that were off the shores of Vietnam, and so the next thing I knew, I got a letter from Tommy from the Sanctuary saying, "Oh, Grandma, you should see this ship. We get clean sheets every day!"

He'd been in the jungle for some weeks. Sure enough, and of course, this was something - obviously, I was raising the money for the Colonial Dames. And he got a ditty bag. We made thousands of ditty bags, little red bags with, you know, some cigarettes and some shaving soap, pads, letter paper, pack of playing cards, things like that for them, so each patient got one of those, and we got letters of course back from the patients and also from the Red Cross girls. So this was really quite an undertaking that the Dames did. We just sort of sponsored those two ships, especially the Sanctuary.

So he finally got home, as I told you, and he settled down as a lawyer in Texas.

Q: Since you mentioned the Colonial Dames, tell me about your presidency.

Streeter: Oh. Well. Yes. The Dames, I think I told you, had presented me with a stand of colors when I was a major at the time, director of the Marine Corps Women's Reserve, which I have since returned to the Marine Corps and they are in the museum there, and these, the Marine Corps colors, you know, they have a sort of ribbon which ways "U.S. Marine Corps" on it, United States Marine Corps; they were allowed, by disposition of the Commandant, General Holcomb, to put Women's Reserve U.S. Marine Corps on this, and they're the only colors that have this writing on them, because shortly afterwards, a regulation was made that only the combat units could have the name of the unit on the Marine Corps flag. So the only one that has the "Women's Reserve" on it is the one which the Colonial Dames gave to me.

So I was national president of the Dames from '48 to '52, and then I have always been, you know, tied in with them since, and I did raise this money for the Vietnam War and all of that. I'm very fond of them, and I visited a great many of the historic houses which they have restored in the various states, and that led to my interest in historic houses in and around Morristown later on. But that has been a very pleasant connection.

Q: You were president from 1948 to '52.

Streeter: Yes. Then also –

Q: By virtue of your ancestry?

Streeter: I had been a member before, you see. But I was national president; they each have a state president too. Then at the same time I was made a governor of the Colony Club in New York, and I was for twelve years a governor of the Colony Club, which I enjoyed very much.

Q: That entailed a lot of –

Streeter: Yes, that was quite a lot of work. It was quite a job, a club like that.

Q: What's the membership of the Colony Club?

Streeter: 2000, something like that. I think it's 1200 residents members and 800 non-resident, something like that, of that sort. I'm sorry, I forget. But that was a very pleasant connection too. And they had a 75th anniversary just last December, in which it was a fashion show. They had all costumes of previous years. So they had one period for the World War II period, and we had one girl who had been Rosie the Riveter, one girl who had been a war correspondent, and a Navy girl who had been in the Paymaster Department so she had to wear a revolver. And we had one girl who'd been a Red Cross girl in World War I, and myself, so we were the group that were in that section of the celebration for the 75th Anniversary.

Q: The Colony Club is just a social club, isn't it?

Streeter: Oh, yes, absolutely.

Q: With a lovely restaurant, I might say.

Streeter: Yes. Well, I was partly responsible for getting air conditioning in the Colony Club. And what we now do, we close the regular restaurant in the summer, and air condition the ballroom. We had to air condition the ballroom, summer or winter, so we have a buffet lunch down in the ballroom in the summer, which is very good. Very much used.

It's been very pleasant for me, because if I want to go in to New York I don't have to stay at a hotel, I can stay at the Club.

And I've just discovered - because they also would like something about my history at the present time - so I'm getting a little overlapping here, but I discovered that there are only forty members of the club who have been members longer than I have. I became a member in 1926. And I remember well our 50th anniversary. That was a fine occasion.

That's before we began allowing gentlemen in the club.

Q: Gentlemen to have membership in the club?

Streeter: No, they don't have membership, but they can come and stay with their wives. And of course they came to the 75th anniversary. They did not come to the 50th anniversary at all.

Q: But they could always come to dinner?

Streeter: Oh, yes, they could come as guests. They could come as guests.

Q: Because I've been there as a guest.

Streeter: Oh, yes. We like to have them come as guests. But now they can stay at the club and all that.

Well, the 50th anniversary was a cozy little party. It was a costume party, and a whole group of us came with Mrs. Junius Morgan, who at that time had become rather portly, so she came as Henry VIII. The rest of us came as all his wives, you see. We had a lively dinner party.

Q: Which wife did you turn out to be?

Streeter: I can't remember. All I remember is I had a

hilarious evening. And after dinner, there was a program, and the program was entitled - oh dear, what was it? Oh yes, "Infamous Moments in the Lives of the Famous." This was a skit put on of course by the members, and that was good. And the gentlemen never got to see that.

Well, you can see, I resumed my social life, as it were, and also I had lots of grandchildren coming and going, all that sort of thing, and this was all very nice and pleasant.

But going back to the double life, which I told you, I had got in the habit of living -

Q: - and which you rather relished too, I might say, living the double life.

Streeter: Oh, yes. Yes.

Q: And flourished too.

Streeter: Well, you see, as I told you, I had time for it. If I hadn't had time I couldn't have done it but there you are.

So there were several quite interesting things I did then. I told you about the row I got into with the Legion about the veterans' services.

Q: Yes.

Streeter: Then, I was elected, mind you I was elected, I didn't get appointed or anything, but I was voted for, as a delegate to the 1947 New Jersey Constitutional Convention. Thereby hang a whole lot of tales. This is the state constitution, and it had been amended a great many times in the previous 104 years.

Q: The State Constitution?

Streeter: The State Constitution had been. But of course it had become a patchwork quilt, and nobody was satisfied with it the way it was then and they thought it should be overhauled from the beginning, which they were quite right in thinking.

Q: Did it have any glaring defects that had to be remedied?

Streetere: Well, apparently it had so many, and they were sort of contradictory, that the thing didn't make too much sense.

So, they overreached themselves, the people who were interested in that, and they tried, I think in 1944, in the middle of World War II, to rewrite the Constitution.

Now, there are two ways provided in the Constitution for doing that. It can be done by the legislature or it can be done by a special convention. In both cases it must be ratified by a referendum of the people. But they undertook to do it by the legislature, and it was soundly defeated in the referendum, and it was defeated for two reasons. The first and very obvious and sensible one, which I would have thought they could have anticipated, was that so many men were overseas. They were in the service in 1944, and why should they amend the State Constitution when a whole lot of people who were going to be affected by it couldn't possibly express any opinion about it?

So that contributed largely to its defeat. And the other thing which defeated it was, the method of taxation provided for raising state taxes, and thereby hangs a long and devious tale which I will proceed to tell you. There was no particular secret about it at the time, but in those days we had a form of tax on the railroads, and don't ask me exactly what it was but it was different from the tax on other real estate, business property or personal property. It had a different method of taxing. And the method was vastly valuable to Jersey city and Hudson County because they were the termini of the transcontinental railroads. They had these great railroad yards there, and they took up a lot of property and they provided a great many funds for Jersey City. And the new proposed constitution changed the method of taxing those yards, and Jersey City en masse voted against the constitution. For that reason.

Q: That was a pretty potent vote, in Hudson County.

Streeter: Oh, this was in the days of Mayor Hague, his heyday.

Q: That vote, as a I recall, was always withheld until the count was far advanced, and then they –

Streeter: I don't think they even needed to, this time. The current was so obvious. So anyhow, I wasn't here, of course, I was in Washington, but the 1944 draft of the Constitution was overwhelmingly defeated for those two reasons. Nevertheless it was a sound idea. So, having learned from some experience, they waited till 1947, by which time the soldiers were all back home again and could vote, so that objection was out of the way. But there was still the knotty question of what was to be done with taxing the Jersey City railroad yards.

So they had a vote, a whole ballot and whole election, to vote for something like 90 delegates. The delegates were based on the number of assemblymen plus the two state senators, and for instance, we had two assemblymen and one state senator in Morris County, so we got three votes. Jersey City got a great many more, and so did Newark and all the larger countires. So there were ninety in all, and about nine women, I should say, were among the elected delegates, and this constitutional convention was duly set up and elected and put to work.

The sessions were held in the gymnasium of Rutgers University, which was not air conditioned, and it was a long hot summer, I can tell you, and we worked all summer at it, three days a week generally, and the president of Rutgers,

Dr. Clothier, was president of the convention. Mrs. Katzenbach was vice president, and then there were all the delegates, and the delegates were divided up into committees. There was the judiciary committee and the committee on the executive, committee on the legislative, committee on this and that. And I ended up in the committee on taxation and finance.

Q: That's a hot one.

Streeter: Of course they didn't know where to put me. I didn't know anything about taxation and finance, but then I didn't know much about anything else either, and they put me on the committee on taxation and finance, I think on the theory that I could understand what the situation was and I didn't need to know the details.

So we met solemnly, oh my solemnly, all summer, and we were petitioned and we had postcard ballots, lobbying for this or lobbying against that, and it was a long dull summer, to be perfectly honest about it, considering that we knew what we were sitting on that committee for in the beginning, because obviously we were sitting on that committee so as not to upset Jersey City and Hudson County another time. We were to find a way out of taxation and finance which was going to get the votes of Hudson County for this constitution instead of against it. And we argued and we had public hearings, we went through the whole rigamarole, and then finally we passed a resolution which was submitted to the whole constitutional convention, and it was in due time approved by them.

Well, if you can understand what it is, it's more than I or any or the rest of us could, and we had eminent lawyers, including Mayor Hague's lawyer, and Mr. Milton who was a very suave and intelligent gentleman. We all knew exactly what we were supposed to do, so this was a certain amount of shadow boxing, but never mind.

So anyhow, we brought up this resolution which satisfied Jersey City. That's all we had to do. And it was eventually incorporated and eventually the referendum passed.

I did not particularly distinguish myself. There's no particular way I could. And I just sort of went along with this. It was the obvious thing to do. But then we got down to the last time, and we'd submitted all these resolutions and they'd been amended by the full convention, if somebody had some trouble about it, all the amendments had been voted and finally we got to the last day, and we had provided the previous day, that no changes could be made thereafter on the day that we were going to vote, the last day.

Q: Vote it up or down?

Streeter: We'd chewed all this thing over for weeks. And anybody who wanted amendments had had a chance to put them in, and they'd gone up or down as the constitutional convention voted. But the last day there were to be no amendments except by unanimous consent.

Well, you know, there's always somebody. So this man got up, I've forgotten his name now but it's easy enough to find, and he begged the tolerance of the convention, but he'd been lying awake all night worrying about something, and he did feel that he must propose an amendment. He hoped they would be willing to consider it.

Well, what do you think his amendment was? He thought we were being too hard on traitors!

Q: On what?

Streeter: Traitors. On traitors, yes! I should have looked this up, but I can look it up if you want - the previous constitution provided that treason should consist only in giving aid and comfort to the enemy or in an overt act.

Q: In time of war?

Streeter: Yes. In time of war. And he thought, well, this was bad because in time of war people got hysterical and they accused people of being traitors when they weren't really traitors and they just got carried away. And so he was worrying too much about how we might be hard on traitors.

So hardly had the gentleman sat down, of course, than I leaped to my feet and said he certainly wasn't going to get unanimous consent for that amendment, that I'd always particularly despised traitors - there was no reason why we should go easy on them. They'd got all the protection they deserved and that was that, period.

So there was sort of a hush. Then there was a nice old Scotsman, he was a judge, and he got up and he said, "Well," he thought perhaps he could shed some light on the subject that might avoid too lengthy an altercation. That he thought, after all, the state of New Jersey was unlikely to go to war all by itself, and consequently treason was more likely to be a federal crime than it was to be a state crime, and he thought it was unnecessary to spend too much time on this discussion.

Q: A wise old bird.

Streeter: So then of course the convention laughed its head off and that was the end of that. We went to work and passed the new constitution without any further amendments.

And then of course it went to referendum and it was adopted and we're living under it now. But that's the story. What?

Q: Living happily under it?

Streeter: Oh, I don't know, lawyers never live happily under any constitution. And, oh, they fuss and sputter about it from time to time, but I think on the whole it's stood up pretty well. And some things, the whole legal section was apparently very much better. I didn't of course have too much to do with that. But I knew where my duty was and I've done it, on taxation and finance. You know, that was quite fun.

Well, then there were some other things happened too.

Q: Yes, there were. There was one before the war, World War II, when you were a member of the first Interstate Compacts Commission, which is a mystery to me. That was in 1939.

Streeter: That's right. That was something. Again this was the first one. You see, I've been lucky. I've been on first things quite often, first committees, first things of one sort or another, and this was a new idea which had been now permitted by Congress. See, in the past, if two states had a disagreement about borders, what have you –

Q: Waterways.

Streeter: Yes. It could only be decided by the Congress. It had to go to the Congress. And of course the Congress didn't want to be bothered with it, and of course New Jersey was always arguing about the Delaware with Pennsylvania and Delaware, and well, hot pursuit, for instance. Suppose somebody does a hold up in Trenton, and beats it across the bridge to Pennsylvania? The cops can pursue him but it he gets to Pennsylvania he's all right. And so, Congress finally, in order to relieve itself of a lot of small things of this nature, passed a law saying that states could get together. I don't know if it said ajoining states. It may have. I've forgotten. But anyhow, they could get together and fight out this business for themselves, and the Delaware River has been one of the chief things they have fought about. And any agreement between them, I think probably has to be ratified by Congress - I've forgotten - but they could do all their fighting among themselves first without wasting Congress's time. And I think this was a good idea. I think it probably has worked out well, as far as I know. So that was interesting.

Q: The commission worked that out, as a system.

Streeter: Yes.

Q: Who made the appointments to this commission?

Streeter: Governors made these appointments with the advice and consent of the Senate, the State Senate.

Q: I see.

Streeter: One time the blasted Senate didn't consent, not this time, Interstate Compacts Commission. We'll get to that subject later on.

Well, where are we? I don't want to spend too much time on this, but it just shows that I really didn't come back to a dull time, there was quite a lot —

Q: No, indeed you didn't. Tell me about the Electoral College that you served on.

Streeter: Oh, yes. Well, of course the Electoral College is something that gets threatened with abolition.

Q: It gets lambasted every four years.

Streeter: Oh, and in between. When they've got nothing else to do, they abolish the Electoral College.

Q: But they never seem to achieve it.

Streeter: But they haven't done it. In the early days, there was a real reason for it, because of the difficulty in travel and in communications between the different states. You didn't have radio. You didn't have television. One state didn't know what the other state was doing often until days and weeks after it had happened, and they were not as well informed about each other's problems and the problems of the country as a whole, and so, they agreed to this system, which was to elect members of the Electoral College. Then the Electoral College elected the President.

Occasionally, I think it hasn't worked in accordance with the popular vote, but practically always it has. It would be entirely possible for the Electoral College to make a different decision from the popular vote.

Q: That's the issue they always bring up.

Streeter: That's the issue.

Q: The possibility that it might.

Streeter: And of course, an elector does not have to be bound by the popular vote in his own state. He's elected, for instance I was elected by the Republican Party in New Jersey, but I could have voted for a Democrat if I'd wanted to, once I was elected. The choice of the President is made by the Electoral College, and this is what some people fuss about. Somebody might get bribed or something or other, don't you know. And of course that I think has never happened, I think, or at least very, very seldom. They practically always voted in accordance with the wish of the party that elected them.

I think myself that it might be entirely sensible to have a percentage vote. (Yes, that is an awfully soft sofa, not always as comfortable as it might be —

Q: — this is much better.)

Streeter: Good. For instance, if they vote in New Jersey or New York state 60-40, you could divide the members of the Electoral College 60-40, and in that way you would end probably by getting an accurate reflection of the popular vote.

Q: The will of the people, yes.

Streeter: And I don't think that there would be any great objection to that. I don't know that there's any great advantage to it. You might, I suppose, just as well go from the Electoral College as it is now, out to the popular vote, without an in between step like that. It was a — well, I don't know, but I think it was a little bit a distrust of the popular vote, and a little bit wanting to keep some make weight among the better educated people of the time. I don't know.

Q: Well, that is reflective of history —

Streeter: Yes, it's the English idea, anyhow. But actually I think that by and large, the Electoral College gives people a chance to sit down and think about it, you know. It doesn't meet till a little while after the vote. If something went asbolutely haywire in the popular vote, you've got a recourse. Whether it would ever work if you tried to work it, I don't know - whether, if the Electoral College chose a person who did not have a majority of the popular vote, I don't know whether he could ever swing it as President. So I think it's extremely unlikely to happen, but there have been cases where it's been very, very close. The Electoral College vote has been close or the popular vote has been close. And it's a period of uncertainty.

Q: It's an anachronism, and yet -

Streeter: I think it is in a way sort of entertaining, that no matter how logically they try to upset it, it never has been upset.

Now, it didn't amount to a hill of beans, I'm sorry to say. There was no great enthusiasm about this.

Q: This was in 1948?

Streeter: Yes. I wish I had that ballot because my name is on it, one of fourteen electors, they voted for me, see, not for Mr. Dewey in New Jersey.

Well, then we simply went down to the State House in Trenton, on an occasion when we were all together, and we cast the fourteen votes of New Jersey for Mr. Dewey. And that's all. Then they were mailed down to Washington where they were snowed under by the votes for Mr. Truman. On the whole I think Mr. Truman was a much better president than Mr. Dewey would have been, so I'm well in favor of anything, the Electoral College gets set back, if that's what people really want. But I'm always interested to see it come up. It's an old hardy annual. It comes up every time after an election, and nobody does anything about it. So we've still got it.

And it was an interesting experience. Now, I did not go to that election in Washington. I didn't realize that the losing electors were - really got to get invitations to everything, just as much as the winning ones.

Q: You mean to the Inauguration?

Streeter: Yes. So I didn't. I had some other plans at that time, so I didn't go to that Inauguration, but I've been to other ones so I know what it's like.

Well, that was sort of fun, but it was again more trappings than it was actual.

Q: Trappings of our democracy, the peculiar trappings of

our democracy -

Streeter: They have their place. I think trappings do. Now, let's see - we're getting along pretty well. I think I'm growing up, as you might say. There was a time that I thought I was never going to get beyond seventeen in this oral history!

Q: A most interesting assignment - the federal grand jury.

Streeter: Oh, yes, this was wonderful.

Q: This was in 1953-54, in Newark, New Jersey.

Streeter: Yes. Now, this really was something.

Q: Did you know what you were getting into when you served on this?

Streeter: No. Nobody would tell me, because they're not supposed to tell me. You're supposed to use your own common sense. However, this was very interesting. Of course I was drawn. My name was drawn in the first place by somebody down there in Newark. They have lists. Then I was appointed foreman by Judge Richard Hartshorn, whom I knew. By this time I was getting to know quite a lot of people around New Jersey.

Q: Yes, I would think you would.

Streeter: He was a very fine man. So he appointed me foreman and he appointed a Mr. Shelton clerk, and those were the only two officers of the grand jury.

Q: How many members on the grand jury?

Streeter: Twenty-three on a grand jury, and it takes twelve to bring in a true bill, an indictment.

Well, I didn't know anything about it. Tom was a lawyer of course, but they - he never was a trial lawyer. Of course he knew about grand juries but he didn't tell me very much about it. I went to see Judge Hartshorn, and said, "Look, Sir, what do I do about this? I don't know how to be foreman of a federal grand jury or any grand jury."

He said, "I'm not going to tell you, because you're supposed to exercise your own native wit.

So then I went to Judge Augustus Hand, who was an old friend of mine, in New York.

Q: Is he related to Learned Hand?

Streeter: Yes, he was a cousin, I think, of Learned Hand but they were both on the same court, and it was Gus that I knew, so I went to see him. He couldn't have been more amused. Our middle son Henry had been his law clerk at one time, and he said, "Well, now, that's great fun, and I'm awfully glad to see you, and let's go down and listen to what my fellow justices are doing for this afternoon," so we went down and listened to Judge Medina and some of the rest of them here on a very dull case, and I said, "That's fine, Judge, I'm awfully glad to see this, but what do I do about a grand jury?"

"Well," he said, "you can't expect me to tell you. We don't tell grand jurors what to do. That's the whole point. They're supposed to make up their own minds about things. This is your peers, you know, a jury of your peers."

"Well," I said, "a big help you two are."

And so anyhow we started to organize. The prosecutor was there, Mr. W. F. Thompkins, and he was very good, and he had a lot of young helpers, assistant prosecutors who were from some of the big law firms. Jimmy Pitney was one of them. So we had an easy case. Somebody had dumped some mail down, you know, a chute - a gutter - so this was no great brain drain. They went out. And the clerk started to call the roll. So he began with me. Well, I wish you could have heard the riot - "Well, who does she think she is?"

Q: From the other jurors?

Streeter: From the other jurors. "Why should she vote first? Does she think we're all going to vote the way she votes?"

Q: Already, they knew you were foreman, so -

Streeter: So this young riot was going on, on the floor, you see. I listened for a little while, and finally - I was sitting up on the dias, you know, with a great big desk in front of me and a gavel. So finally I whacked the gavel and I said, "Now, ladies and gentlemen, let's have a little quiet. I have a suggestion to make. I've always found that I'm in a very desirable position because my name begins with S, and I suggest that we vote alphabetically. This is very helpful to me, because by the time you get down to S, I'll see which way the cat's going to jump and then I can vote accordingly."

So that settled that. We voted alphabetically.

Q: That took the onus off you.

Streeter: Oh my, I defused that bomb very easily. Well, we had a very interesting time. It was a nice bunch. We had about two of everything, every race, I should think, and every religion.

Q: How many women?

Streeter: About nine women I think were on it, a number of women. Some were educated people. Some were not educated people. But it was a good selection, I mean, if you believe in the grand jury system, and I do, you had a good cross-section.

Q: Were you confined for a certain period?

Streeter: Oh, yes. Well, we weren't locked up, except of course the days we met. We met three days a week for about seven months, I think. And our deliberations were private. The prosecutor wasn't there during the deliberations at all.

Well, the first thing we had to do, and I found it difficult too, to begin with, we all couldn't understand why we didn't hear both sides of the question. You see? We'd always heard about juries, the way we think of them as petty juries, you've got to hear both sides of the question to decide what's right. But we weren't a petty jury, we were a grand jury, and a grand jury doesn't hear the other side of the case. All a grand jury is supposed to do is find out whether there is "probable cause" that a crime has been committed. "Probable cause." In other words, just because I say so and so killed my dog or something like that, that doesn't necessarily mean that he did. Maybe somebody just ran over him accidentally or something. There's got to be enough evidence shown to the grand jury to get a prosecutor a case to make before a petty jury. Not just, you know, malicious gossip or something of that sort.

So it took us a week or so to get that idea through our heads. We all, including me, were inclined to think, "Well, where's the guy on the other side, his representative? We don't see anybody around to give us any idea of how he feels about it."

Q: Who imparted this point to the jury?

Streeter: Oh yes, we'd been told all this.

Q: The prosecutor was the one who laid it forth to you?

Streeter: Yes. Oh, I think so, yes. Certainly the judge had made the point to me, both judges. I mean, really, if we'd stopped to think, we would have known, and that's why it's a different number of people, and that's why a majority vote, you see - one person can't hold up an indictment. It's by majority vote. So you hear one side of the case, and you try to say, well, now, when the petty jury listens to this guy testify, is he credible? Is he telling the truth? We listened to some of the biggest liars I ever saw in my life, and I knew perfectly well they were lying. But I swore them in and they solemnly lied with a straight face. You get sometimes to have a feel of it, I think, as to who's telling the truth and who isn't. Well -

Q: Such lies are not subject to charge of perjury?

Streeter: Oh, no, not before a grand jury. I don't think. At least we didn't try to. We just made up our own minds, whether we'd believe them or not.

So, they broke us in gradually, and then, we got to Albert Anastasia. Well, Albert Anastasia was in the public press, called - the head of Murder, Incorporated. And the theory was that when the Mafia in New York wanted to bump off somebody in St. Louis, why, they didn't bother to do it themselves, they got ahold of Albert and he sent a hatchet man out to bump him off. This was all perfectly well known, as you might say. But of course we couldn't indict him for murder because murder is a state crime. And none of the states ever had the nerve to try and indict Albert for murder. So he was running around the streets perfectly respectably.

Q: Supervising other murders.

Streeter: Oh, yes. Yes. Well, of course, the only thing we could indict him for was income tax evasion. So we went to work on that.

This, of course, had by this time been reduced pretty much to a formula. It was the only weapon that the federal courts had, and they knew how to go about it.

Well, Albert and his family had arrived in this country such and such a year, I've forgotten what, saying that they had no money. They were immigrants and they had no money, just enough to get here, like many others. Then time went by, time went by and Albert prospered, and he built himself a mansion in Fort Lee. Sort of a palace.

Q: Roman Palace.

Streeter: Yes. And so we got in all the people, the general contractor who built it, the people who had furnished it, the furniture people, the wallpaper people, the carpet people, and they all brought in the bill of the goods that they had furnished for this mansion. And it came of course to a good many thousand dollars, which they had paid no income tax on all these years. They must have had the money or they couldn't have built the house.

So, it looked as if this was a good case of income tax evasion. Well, we had Tough Tony, Albert's brother, who was the boss of the dock workers, from Brooklyn, and he was a witness about something or other to do with it. Well, they all said, "Yes," they'd been paid, but they didn't know who had paid them. Most of them said they'd not been paid by check. They'd been paid by a man who gave them the cash. And they didn't know who the man was, no, they had no idea who the man was, except there was one witness who was the general contractor, and he said, yes, he had been paid by a man whom he knew to be Albert Anastasia.

So that of course put the finger on Albert. So he was the chief witness and we believed him. So we brought in an indictment against Albert.

Q: Did you have Albert himself on the stand?

Streeter: No, no, the grand jury never has the —

Q: — not the principal ones.

Streeter: Not the principal one. Just his brother, who had some connection, I've forgotten just what, with it.

So later on, Albert was tried, and because of this witness, who said, "Yes, I was paid and I know it was Albert Anastasia who paid me," he was convicted of income tax evasion.

Well, then, of course, there were a few weeks. It was around Christmas time, I think, and this contractor had retired by this time. He was an older man. He retired, and he and his wife had a little cottage down in Florida, and what happened was that he disappeared. He and his wife disappeared. The cottage was found covered with blood. No bodies were ever found. There was no corpus delicti. They disappeared. Every sign of the place having been ransacked and their being murdered. And after all, for the head of Murder, Inc. his was just an afternoon's fun.

Well, I give Tommy Thompkins cards and spades, he went to Anastasia's lawyer and he said, "Now, look here. I'm going to try your client again and he'll certainly be hanged higher than a kite if you ever let this go to trial again, after this thing having happened," and he bluffed Anastasia's lawyer into pleading guilty of income tax evasion. Not to murder, to income tax evasion. And of course my theory is that if it had ever gone to any jury again, they'd have been too frightened —

Q: — to do anything about it —

Streeter: — to make him guilty. But they scared his lawyer into having him plead guilty, and he went to federal prison for about a year. That's about all he got for income tax evasion. And when he came out, remember, there was the great meeting of the Mafia up in Bergen County, they got raided by the state police?

Q: Oh, yes.

Streeter: Gangsters from all over the country.

Q: Yes, somewhere in the country (Appalachia) —

Streeter: They had met to redesign their lordships, you know, their kingdoms, and now that Albert was back, just how was this all going to work out?

Well, how it worked out was that Albert was running around loose for a while, and went to the barber to get shaved one day and somebody came in and shot him in the barber chair, you remember.

Q: Yes. That was in New York City, I think.

Streeter: Yes. So - this is what happened to Albert. And we started the wheels turning that brought him to his bad end.

Well, he never will be missed. So that was the end of Albert.

Q: Was there any sense of fear within the jury?

Streeter: Any what?

Q: Sense of fear, within your - ?

Streeter: None. I told you, I asked my husband and he said "Oh, no, grand jurors don't need to be worried. Nobody's going to bother them. They'd have to bother twelve of them to get them to change their vote. They only have to bother one petty juror, so they'll just save their time for him."

Q: How did the word leak out to Murder, Inc. that this

contractor said yes, it had been - ?

Streeter: Oh, I don't think it leaked. It came out in public. We indicted him. We figured there was sufficient evidence to make a case against him. We didn't say what the evidence was. But when the case came before the petty jury, the witness came out and testified. You see.

Q: Was there not any effort to protect him, as a result of his testimony?

Streeter: Apparently not. Apparently not.

Q: That ought to follow as an obligation, should it not?

Streeter: Of course you can't tell. There was never any bodies found. And it could have been that they were spirited off somewhere and all this mess left to give the Mafia the feeling that he'd been killed. See, I mean wheels within wheels.

The old contractor and his wife may be living happily under a different name somewhere else, like, you know, your OSS people.

Well, then we had another racketeer case, and that was Longy Zwillman, and Longy Zwillman was a different sort of a character from Albert. He'd been a bootlegger, and he had a nice side to him. He was a prosperous bootlegger, and in the depths of the Depression he ran a soup kitchen in the slums of Newark. He fed a lot of people. So Longy had a lot of supporters.

But I think that Longy also had political ambitions, and it looked to us very much as if Longy was getting public officials under his thumb.

Q: Where did he live, Newark?

Streeter: Yes. That's where he operated anyhow. And this of course is very, very bad. It's more insidious than killing people, is getting their - blackmailing public officials. I can't say definitely that he did, but there was enough evidence to think that there was a tie, and so we felt that, if we could catch Longy Zwillman doing what he hadn't ought to do, it would be better to eliminate him.

So anyhow we voted a true bill against him, for income tax evasion. There was enough evidence to income tax evasion, but the other feeling was a little bit in the picture too, I think probably, as far as I was concerned. So they brought him up on income tax evasion, and he got a hung jury. But then it was found later that he'd bribed a juror. Well, income tax evasion or not income tax evasion, bribing a juror is a crime. So he was of course going to be tried again for bribing a joror, so Longy went and hanged himself in his cellar. And that was the end of Longy.

I think at least we helped to eliminate two undeserving citizens of New Jersey. It's a lot more interesting than people who mishandle the United States mail or something like that.

Q: Yes, indeed, rather exciting, I would say.

Streeter: It was.

Q: These were the two major cases.

Streeter: Yes.

Q: Were there minor ones that you considered also?

Streeter: Oh, yes, all the time. All the time.

Q: They kept you busy with the docket.

Streeter: Oh, yes, I tell you, it was about three days a week for seven months probably. This took a lot of time, and we got $8 a day or something.

Q: How many indictments did you bring in?

Streeter: I couldn't tell you. Some of them were very quick and easy, and others were difficult.

We had a nice policeman come in one day, nice honest police man, came in in uniform. He had his gun with him. I said, "Officer, may I ask you to leave your gun outside the courtroom?"

Very much flustered, he removed his gun. Then he came back in. He'd been traffic cop outside of a school, and there was a little system going on wherever it was, Newark I guess, in those days whereby people hijacked trucks full of goods, you see.

Q: They do it now too.

Streeter: Yes, and they just drove them off.

Q: When they stopped for a coffee break or something.

Streeter: Yes. Well, anyhow, this truck had been busy at some place on the same block as the cop was. He hadn't paid too much attention because, you know, people will have a furniture van in front of their house from time to time. But then as the van was pulling out, the driver stopped and handed him a $20 bill or something like that, didn't say anything, just handed him the $20 bill. Nice honest cop, a $20 bill and his eyes popped out of his head, and he called, I think it was a Catholic school, called the sister and said, "What do I do with this?"

The sister said, "Take it down to the police station and tell them." So she handled the traffic apparently while he went down to the police station and told them that he'd been bribed. Then he came and told us that he'd been bribed, and we were very sympathetic to him. Oh, dear —

Q: It doesn't sound like New York's finest, but —

Streeter: Well, in any case, he was honest. So we had all kinds of things like that.

Well, we had the Jehovah's Witnesses too, you see, because Jehovah's Witness all tried to say — a Jehovah's Witness belives they are all ministers, you see, each individual, and so they tried to use that as an excuse for not being drafted, and fortunately we had a Supreme Court ruling on that, that ministers who are not to be drafted are only graduates of recognized theological schools or something like that.

Q: We have of course the doctrine, the priesthood of all believers. Comparable, I suppose.

Streeter: So that was all very interesting.

Q: That really took up your time, did it not?

Streeter: Oh, it really took it all up, I'll tell you. And I think that's about the last really exciting thing I did. Then I've been in semi-retirement since then.

Q: You belong to various historical associations.

Streeter: Yes.

Q: What contribution did you make there?

Streeter: Well, these things were going on, more or less, you see, up until about the 1960s, and Tom died in '65, and then the next five years really was spent —

Q: Liquidating his —

Streeter: — liquidating his estate and having all the auctions. So, I was pretty busy at home and all, and I did things around Morristown. But after Tom's death I got very much interested in Speedwell Village up here, which is the home of the Vail family, and young Alfred Vail, son of the old ironmaster Stephen Vail, was really a junior partner of Samuel F. B. Morse in the development of the telegraph, something that Morse never really quite admitted, but we have a good deal of documentation on it.

Morse had the idea of the telegraph, and we've never tried to question that. He was an artist, as you know. He was not a scientist ever. And he had a good deal of scientific help from his colleagues when he was a professor at New York University.

Finally, he had put together a very elaborate and delicate machine, which however did work in transmitting by electromagnetism sounds which could be identified and put into words.

Q: Morse Code.

Streeter: And he had an exhibit, a demonstration of it at New York University one September. And one of the students at New York University was Alfred Vail, and he did go to this, and Alfred had worked in his father's iron works here in Morristown. He was a very good mechanic, technician. He could see the possibilities of Morse's telegraph, but he could also see the difficulties with the fragile machine that had been constructed.

Furthermore, Morse was broke, and we have a copy of the agreement between them, which was entered into within three weeks of this demonstration, which in effect makes Alfred Vail a junior partner of Morse. He is to put up the money, to develop the telegraph. He's to work on it on his own place, his father's place, and he's to get a certain share, I think it's a third of the returns in this country and half of any returns of foreign patents.

Actually, the Vails paid for Morse's patents, but Morse didn't give them very much credit for their help in the early days.

Anyhow --

Q: Did they reap some money from it, however?

Streeter: No, not much. The Vails didn't reap any and I don't think Morse ever got much, because it got all mixed up with Congress and a lot of crooked people one way and another. However, the early work on the telegraph was done right here in Morristown, in a barn on the Vail estate, which is now a national landmark, not just a national registry, it's a national landmark. And it's open to the public and it's been quite well restored, so that is something that has taken up a great deal of my time.

I'm also a trustee of the Macculloch Hall Historical Museum, in Morristown, and the New Jersey Historical Society. I was a member of the first New Jersey Historic Sites Council, which was 1968-71, and oh yes, I was a member of the United States Commission for the New Jersey Tercentennary Celebration, which I think was 1968. Now, this is the finest and biggest commission I've got, it's signed by President Eisenhower and countersigned by the Livingston Merchant, whom I knew, or knew in those days, and it's very fine and dandy, but it's one of the things that didn't go very well, because it was at the same time as the New York World's Fair. And New Jersey wanted to have a very fancy building, with a fancy exhibit at the New York World's Fair, so it wouldn't give us any money and neither would it allow us to raise any.

We were very hopeful about this, but we were not able to do very much of anything, because we couldn't get any money from anybody.

Q: What sort of plans had you formulated?

Streeter: Well, what we had formulated was, the march of the French troops from Newport through Morristown, down to Virginia. They came right through here, you know. This is something that Mrs. Brown has written a book about. It was quite important. And we did get a descendant of the Marquis de Lafayette, who's allowed to use the name, apparently, although he's on the distaff side, and we did get him to come here to dinner and we had a little do about it. But we never could have any money. We were going to have a parade. We were going to have all kinds of things. We couldn't get any money from Congress. We couldn't get any money from the state. And the state wouldn't let us go out and ask for money from people, because it wanted to put all its money into this New Jersey pavilion at the New York World's Fair.

Streeter #4 - 359

So I must say, I thought that was rather a disappointment.

Q: It died a-borning then, didn't it?

Streeter: It did. Yes. I told you, I didn't win always.

Q: That was one you didn't.

Streeter: That was one that never really hatched out.

Q: Aren't you or weren't you on the Commission for National Monuments too, Historical Monuments?

Streeter: I don't think so. Oh, then I did get a very nice medal from the American Scenic and Historic Preservation Society. This was in 1972.

Q: Yes, and the occasion for that?

Streeter: Well, just my - I think it was really mostly my work at Speedwell.

Q: Then you had some problems with what is called Patriot's Path?

Streeter: Yes, well, I'll tell you about that.

Q: Tell me about that.

Streeter: Yes. Oh, I nearly forgot to tell you about my latest baby, which has taken a long time growing up. It's called Patriot's Path, and it is what is described as a linear path along the Whippany River. This has been an idea in the minds of a great many people for eight or ten years, I should think, and two or three people - Miss Matilda Frelinghuysen and Mrs. Jarvis Cromwell and myself - gave some land along the river, to be used just as a bicycle path and a linear park, to connect the town of Morristown with the areas to the northeast of us and also the areas to the west of us. It will be twenty-seven miles long when it is all finished, but of course we've got about seven or eight different municipalities, each of them has to raise the money and buy the land and build the pathway, and then it will probably be turned over to the Morris Park Commission to be maintained and policed.

Q: The Whippany River which is the river which runs through your property and their property?

Streeter: That's right. And this has run into all kinds of complications and shortages of money and too much drainage and things of that sort, and going down to Trenton and getting permission from the environmental commission down there.

But in any case, Morris Township in which I live has now completed two large sections that are paved and the county park has two other sections which are gravel, and it's about a three mile stretch, and it connects with Morristown at Speedwell Lake. And it's just about, it's being used now and it's about ready to be formally opened, and I think that when that is really in operation, I'm going to call it a day.

Q: Part of it will run right through your property here?

Streeter: It's on the other bank now.

Q: On the opposite bank.

Streeter: On the opposite bank. Well, there's one more thing I would like to say, if I haven't talked to you too much already.

Q: I think you'd better include that by all means.

Streeter: This is called "Acknowledgements." I have observed that it is customary for authors to thank the various people who have helped them to write a book. And these acknowledgements are usually found either in the introduction or the conclusion. So you can put them wherever you like. Location is less important than the fact of expressing one's gratitude, and this is especially true in my case, because my story has spanned a changing era, during which I was able to lead a double life. I cannot be much help to anybody as a 'role model' because present circumstances are not the same. During most of the time, I was able to make a home and bring up a family and still engage in outside volunteer activities, because we always had a household staff. Sometimes I thought their comings and goings resembled a revolving door, but at least I never prepared my own meals until I was 70 years old! Although I'm now 83 and have lived alone in my little cottage these last 13 years, I'm still able to rely when necessary on a priceless jewel who helps me on occasions. She and her family have lived in an apartment over our old garage for over 50 years. Her son and daughter grew up there, and her grandchildren and great-grandchildren are frequent visitors. To keep up the grounds and generally maintain the lawns, woods and swimming pool, I rely on a former sergeant in the German Army who fought for five years in World War II, but is now an American citizen and has worked here for more than 30 years. In addition, my husband's former secretary has given me a great deal of her time, to keep up my correspondence, and his former accountant answers questions from the Internal Revenue Service for me. Without all these helping hands at home, I could never have found the time to engage in the varied activities which I've recorded in in this history, and I appreciate their cooperation and thank them for it.

"In a wider field, I owe incalculable gratitude to many many people, such as, first, my ancestors, from whom I inherited excellent health and endurance, a New England conscience, for whatever that is worth, and a liberal share of this world's goods. Second, my mother, who provided a happy home, a wide experience, all the 'advantages' and much good advice during my childhood and youth. Third, my husband, who provided another happy home for the 48 years of our married life, and who gave me love, kindness, generosity, considerable understanding and a great deal of patience. Fourth, our children, who were fun in their childhood, and in whom we took pride in their prime, on whom I can now rely if needed, and who have provided us with seventeen grandchildren and three great-grandchildren.

"Fifth, all the friends and loyal supporters who have given me encouragement and lent their talents to the many and varied activities which are recorded here. Such successes as I have had have always been the work of many hands. A large part of any commendations I have received belongs to them. They warmed the cockles of my heart and I thank them for their generosity.

"Sixth, some unknown benefactor who gave my name to Mrs. Patricia King, Director of the Arthur and Elizabeth Schlesinger Library at Radcliffe College, and to Mrs. King who passed me along to Mrs. Elizabeth B. Mason, associate director of the Oral History Research Office of Columbia University. And to Mrs. Mason, who persuaded her husband, Mr. John T. Mason, Jr. director of oral history, U.S. Naval Institute, Annapolis, Maryland, who listened to me talk about myself for hours. I felt secretly ashamed of myself for being so voluble, but he was encouraging and patient, so that I really had fun. I hope anyone who reads these stories will have fun also."

"Some of the grandchildren I have mentioned above have now finished college, and gone out into the wide, wide world. I watch them with admiration and considerable amount of awe. They are growing up in a world very different from the one in which I lived 50 or 60 years ago. In particular, the relations between the sexes have changed markedly. I do believe that women can do well many, though not all, of the things that men have done traditionally, and in these ways they find some fulfillment, but at about age 30 they are in a quandary. They are just getting good at their jobs, but if they would like a family also, they may have to make the choice, for a few years at least, and this can be a problem.

"Somebody once said to me, 'You seem to have come pretty close to having your cake and eating it too.' I think that is true, and it was not a hard choice for me, because circumstances were so unusual, and because my husband was understanding. My family interests always came first, except during World War II, when I was away from home for nearly three years. My husband and our teenage daughter took very good care of each other during that period, when many millions of other Americans had to make a similar choice. It was my great good fortune to have served in the Marine Corps during a time when our country desperately needed the help of all her citizens. Although I never had but one professional job, I could have hoped for nothing better than that, and I am grateful to the Marine Corps and to those who recommended me to their attention.

"I wish I could say that I thought my grandchildren would have no problems, but I'm afraid the clouds are thickening around us. Nevertheless I was startled to have a 25 year old granddaughter say to me the other day, 'No one of my generation expects to live to be 40.' I could hardly blame her, what with nuclear bombs and all, but I said, 'That's no way to talk. You are just letting yourself be licked before you start. You should have heard what we were taught at home, by church and school as well as home.' Everybody said it so we had to believe it was true, and it went like this: 'No one can tell what the future will bring, of joy or sorrow, good times or bad, but what you bring to meet the future, that is within your own pow'r.'"

Or, as my dear old grandmother used to say, "Count your blessings, honey, count your blessings."

Q: That's a great, fine statement.

Streeter: That's the end of that.

Q: And I do thank you, Mrs. Streeter, for all this time you've given us.

Streeter: Well, I thank you. I was just saying to Mrs. Mason, you are most patient and kind and you don't fluster the person you're interviewing, and you do probably get them to tell you things that they hadn't intended to tell you; so I hope that this had been not only an interesting but a pleasant experience for both of us!

Q: Yes, I feel the same way about it.

Index to

Series of Interviews with

Colonel Ruth Cheney Streeter
USMCWR (Retired)

ABELL, Senator Frank: New Jersey State Senator who served as first president of the Morris County Welfare Board, p. 119-20;

AVIATION: comments on women in the Marine Corps and aviation, p. 255-7; also 263;

BOOK COLLECTION OF THOMAS STREETER: p. 310-14;

BRYN MAWR: Ruth Cheney studies latin in Paris as preparation for entry to Bryn Mawr College, p. 26-27; p. 53-4; planned to stay in college for only two years, p. 54-9; becomes V.P. of freshman class, p. 59-60; used her college experience to assess her capabilities, p. 60-61; additional activities, p. 62-3; becomes President of her class - after being out of college for three years - holds that office for next 39 years, p. 65-6; takes part in 50th Anniversary celebration of College, p. 67; chill over relations with Bryn Mawr and other colleges in WW II because of institutional fear of losing undergrads to war effort, p. 68 ff; the 75th anniversary of college, p. 72 ff; Streeter contributes idea for raising money to build dormitories, p. 73; Streeter becomes chairman of Alumnae Day Committee, p. 74;

BUCKLEY, Will and Aloise: (parents of William and James Buckley) - Will was an usher at Streeter wedding - he and Tom Streeter in oil business in Mexico, p. 97; p. 100;

CAMP LEJEUNE: see entries under: U. S. MARINE CORPS WOMEN'S RESERVE.

CHENEY AWARD: given by Cheney Family in memory of Bill Cheney, brother of Mrs. Streeter, p. 84; Mrs. Streeter awarded a plaque in recognition of her service in connection with award, p. 296 ff;

CHENEY, Mary Ward Lynn (Mrs. Charles P.): her marriage to Professor Henry Schofield of Harvard, p. 22; their stay in Berlin and Paris, p. 23-24; attends coronation of George V, p. 28; p. 31-32; her interest in church architecture leads her to build gothic church in Peterborough, NH p. 33; her other interests - nursery school, p. 33; politics and public service, p. 38;

CIVIL AIR PATROL: p. 168; Mrs. Streeter learns to fly in 1940 with intention of contributing to war effort, p. 169; ineligible as a woman to fly with the patrol off the Atlantic Coast p. 172; her comments on learning to fly, p. 174-8; p. 185;

COCHRAN, Jacqueline (Jackie) (Mrs. Floyd Odlum): p. 181-2;

COLONIAL DAMES OF AMERICA: Mrs. Streeter was president from 48-52, p. 319-30;

COLONY CLUB: Mrs. Streeter serves as a governor of Club for twelve years, p. 321; her role in 75th anniversary celebration (Dec. 1958), p. 321; the 50th anniversary party with Mrs. Junius Morgan as Henry VIII, p. 323;

U. S. DEFENSE ADVISORY COUNCIL: p. 294-5;

DRISCOLL, The Hon. Alfred E.: Governor of New Jersey, names Mrs. Streeter to Veteran's Council, p. 285 ff; p. 290; p. 292;

DRYDEN, Major Marion: head woman officer in Marine Corps Aviation Section -- accompanies Mrs. Streeter on Hawaii trip (Oct. 1944), p. 263;

EDISON, Charles: p. 112-3;

EISENHOWER, General Dwight David: his retirement ceremony at the Pentagon, p. 294-5;

ELECTORAL COLLEGE: Mrs. Streeter named in 1948, p. 334 ff;

FEDERAL GRAND JURY: Mrs. Streeter serves in Newark (1953-4), p. 339 ff; Judge Hartshorn names her foreman, p. 339 ff; the case of Albert Anastasia, p. 345 ff; the case of Longy Zwillman, p. 350 ff;

GREAT DEPRESSION OF THE 1930s: p. 108 ff; p. 119 ff; p. 303-6; praise for the work of the Civilian Conservation Corps, p. 306;

HAWAII: assignment of women marines to Hawaii, p. 260 ff;

HISTORICAL SOCIETIES: Mrs. Streeter's activities in this area, p. 357 ff;

HOBBY, Colonel Oveta Culp: first head of WACS, p. 198; p. 261-2;

HOG ISLAND: WW I project of American International Corporation, p. 90;

HOLCOMB, General Thomas: Commandant Marines, p. 197; p. 201;

INDIA: Mrs. Streeter's mother - Mrs. Cheney, visits India, p. 20-21;

INTERSTATE COMPACTS COMMISSION: Mrs. Streeter serves (1939), p. 332-3;

JUNIOR LEAGUE: offshoot of the Sewing Circles, p. 43-4; Streeter proposes a Chapter of the Junior League for Morristown, p. 44-45;

KNOX, The Hon. Frank: Secretary of the Navy, p. 201-4;

LE JEUNE, Miss Eugenia: p. 242; p. 255;

LITTLE GREEN HOUSE ON K STREET: p. 91-2; Streeter home in wartime Washington (WW I) - p. 91-2; they take in two couples to help ease housing shortage, p. 92-5;

MANNING, Mrs. Helen Taft: p. 74-5;

U. S. MARINE CORPS WOMEN'S RESERVE: Mrs. Streeter gives up flying when commissioned in the Marines, p. 185-7; Mrs. Streeter's efforts to find some fruitful outlet for her war effort just prior to enrollment in the Marines, p. 190 ff; Mrs. Streeter's three sons already in the service of the country, p. 192; interview with General Holcomb, Commandant, p. 201-2; sworn in as Director of the Women's Reserves (Feb. 13, 1943) p. 205; her good relations with the press corps, p. 205; Mrs. Streeter on the original intent for a Director of the Women's Marine Corps Reserve, p. 207 ff; correspondence twenty years later, p. 212-3; her contribution of ideas for development of Corps, p. 215; Mrs. Streeter submits first annual report on the Reserves - report rejected, p. 215-6; no responsibility - no authority, p. 217-8; frustration, p. 219-20; Streeter conducts her office with dignity, military efficiency and humanity, p. 223-4; role of the chaplain's corps, p. 228-30; recruiting trips, p. 233-8; Streeter goes aloft with paratroopers making their first jump, 240-1 ff; further introduction to the rigors of training at Camp LeJeune, p. 241 ff; enlistments in Women's Corps in first eight weeks, p. 248; the home town platoon, p. 249-50; the women at Camp LeJeune, p.250 ff; jobs assigned the women, p. 252-3; comments on promotions, p. 254-6; assignment of women marines to Hawaii, p. 259 ff; the Director and communications through channels, p. 274-5; the Marine Corps band, p. 276-8; the seventeen-year olds as officer training aspirants, p. 278-9; Saturday reviews, p. 279-80;

McAFEE, Mildred (Mrs. Douglas Horton): first head of the WAVES, p. 198-9;

McBRIDE, Katharine: President of Bryn Mawr College, p. 71 ff; p. 74-6;

MINTO, Lord: Governor General of Canada, p. 18; Governor General of India, p. 20-21;

MOORE, The Hon. A. Harry: three-term governor of New Jersey, p. 107 ff;

MOORE, Mrs. Paul: calls on Mrs. Streeter in Morristown and asks her to become President of the Morristown Visiting Nurse Association, p. 105-6;

MORRIS COUNTY WELFARE BOARD: Streeter serves during 1932-41; p. 118; succeeds the first head, Senator Abell, and serves for eight years, p. 121;

MORRISTOWN VISITING NURSES ASSOCIATION: p. 105-6;

MORSE, Samuel F. B,.: development of the telegraph - the role played by his young partner Alfred Vail of Morristown, p. 355 ff;

NEW JERSEY CONSTITUTIONAL CONVENTION: Mrs. Streeter elected (1947) as a delegate, p. 325; need for a new constitution - one proposal had been voted down in 1944, p. 325-6; problem was to get a solution that was satisfactory to Hudson County, p. 328-9;

NEW JERSEY STATE BOARD OF CHILDREN'S GUARDIANS: Mrs. Streeter becomes a member, p. 106 ff;

NEW JERSEY STATE RELIEF COUNCIL: Streeter becomes only woman on the Council in 1932-3; p. 109-110; p. 113-4;

NEW JERSEY VETERAN'S COUNCIL: Mrs. Streeter serves on Council from 1946-53, p. 285-94;

O'CONNOR, The Hon. Basil (Doc): p. 160-1; p. 190; p. 196; p. 200;

PATRIOT'S PATH: Mrs. Streeter's role in the development, p. 359-60;

USS SANCTUARY - hospital ship: p. 318; Mrs. Streeter, through the Colonial Dames, had helped with supplies for the ship, p. 319;

SEA BEES - in Hawaii: p. 264;

SEWING CIRCLES: their influence on debuts, etc. p. 41-2; develop into the modern Junior League, p. 43; p. 52-54;

SPEEDWELL VILLAGE: Mrs. Streeter's interest - the role of Alfred Vail in the development of the telegraph, p. 356-7;

STRATTON, Captain Dorothy: first head of the Coast Guard SPARS in WWII, p. 198;

STREETER FAMILY: Post World War II p. 299 ff; the Adirondacks in wartime, p. 309-10; the move from the big house, p. 314; an account of the grandson - Thomas II - his service in Vietnam, p. 315 ff;

STREETER, Colonel Ruth Cheney (Mrs. Thos. W. Streeter, Sr.) USMCWR: background - immediate family, p. 1 ff; memories of Baltimore in the winter, 11 ff; New Orleans, p. 14; Canada, p. 17-18; early education, p. 23; education - Switzerland and Paris, p. 24-30; stepfather, p. 32-3; brothers, p. 35-6; church influence, p. 39; school in Boston, p. 39-40; debut in Boston (1913), p. 40-51; role of the Sewing Circles, p. 41 ff; the ball, p. 46; second debut in Ottawa, p. 46-9; role of her brothers in WW I, p. 77 ff; Younger brother killed in air crash over Foggia, Italy, p. 83-4; resultant Cheney Award, p. 84; her meeting and romance with Thos. W. Streeter, p. 87-90; the move from New York to Morristown, p. 103-4; the financial crash of 1929, p. 104; more on family life in Morristown, p. 124 ff; summer at Dinard in France, p. 134-139; the Adirondacks, p. 139-41; Blue Hill, Maine, p. 142; the great Depression, p. 145-7; flying incident that involved landing in a corn field, p. 149 ff; picture of family life in Morristown, p. 153-4; the Civil Air Patrol career, p. 168 ff; flying, p. 174 ff; she learns difference between fright and panic, p. 183; flying career comes to an end with duty in Marine Corps - the week-end incident, p. 185-7; her comments on mutual cooperation between her husband and herself on career objectives, p. 192-3; her trip to Hawaii in Oct. 1944 as Director of Women Marines, p. 262-70; her philosophy of hard work, p. 270 ff; her award - the Legion of Merit, p. 280; other recognition, p. 280-2; her illness - notice taken by the Commandant, p. 283; her service and experiences on Veteran's Council, p. 285 ff; efforts of some to get a soldier's bonus, she opposed - 287 ff; acknowledgements, p. 361-2;

STREETER, Thomas W. Sr.: p. 87-90; with the American International Corporation in New York, p. 90; his wartime job in Washington (WW I) for Department of Purchases, etc. p. 91 ff; family returns to New York in 1919, p. 96; his business associations with Will Buckley, p. 97-100; a tin mine in Alaska, p. 100 and p. 128; gold leases, p. 100-1; p. 129-31; The move to Morristown, NJ, p. 103-4; settling claims against bankrupt Bank of the U. S., p. 114-115; retires and becomes an historian and book collector, p. 115 ff; also p. 157-162 and p. 310-314; the Cambridge Platform, p. 162 ff; the Pigaffetta, p. 164-5;

TALES OF AN ANCIENT MARINE: privately published by Mrs. Streeter - an account of her years with the Marine Corps, p. 195;

THOMAS, Dr. M. Carey: President of Bryn Mawr College, p. 56;

TOWLE, Col. Katherine A.: Comes into Marine Corps with Col. Streeter as Assistant Director, p. 219; at end of WW II became Assistant Dean of Women at University of California --then back as Director of Women in the Marine Corps after they had become regulars, p. 222; becomes member of Commandant's Staff, p. 222;

TRENTON: see references under:
STATE RELIEF COUNCIL: NEW JERSEY STATE BOARD OF CHILDREN'S GUARDIANS;

WALLER, Brig. Gen. L. W. T., Jr. (USMC - Ret.):
        p. 197-8; p. 200; p. 215; p. 217-18; p. 263; p. 280;
        also entries under:
        <u>STREETER</u>, Col. Ruth Cheney: and
        <u>U. S. MARINE CORPS WOMEN'S RESERVE</u>

WASP'S: (Women's Air Service Pilots): Streeter wanted to fly with them
        -- disbarred because of age, p. 181-2;

WAVES: Mrs. Streeter approaches WAVES to see if they could use a pilot,
        p. 190-1; they undertake early training of the Marine Corps
        women, p. 214; p. 236;

WORLD WAR I: p. 51-2; p. 55; p. 77-86;

www.ingramcontent.com/pod-product-compliance
Lightning Source LLC
Chambersburg PA
CBHW080620170426
43209CB00007B/1477